INSIDER'S
SECRETS
OF
TRAVEL
BARGAINS

VENTURA BOOKS
New York City
Printed in the United States
All Rights Reserved

TABLE OF CONTENTS

I

INTRODUCTION

This travel guide may well be different from any other book you've ever read. It is not designed to tell you which zoos and museums to visit, nor is its purpose to list the best hotels in the capitals of the world. You will not find descriptions of glamorous cruises to enchanted islands, nor will it feature expensive around-the-world packages.

Instead, you'll find it to be exactly the kind of travel guide more and more people so desperately need: A guide designed to save you money. Simply put, this guide allows the average person or family to go on a real vacation at realistic prices. The money saved will be substantial: in fact, it may mean an extra three days in the country of your choice, and it will definitely get you out of the backyard pool and off to a real vacation. In any case, you'll have learned how to prevent inflation from ruining your vacation hopes and plans this year.

You probably have had a friend, family member, or maybe even your doctor, tell you that you need a vacation. In response, you may have packed your bags and headed off to the Caribbean Islands, Europe, California, or Japan. More likely, you wanted to take off on such a trip, but in reality, you stayed at home, moaning about prices which prevented you from leaving.

If you were one of the lucky ones who did not suffer from prices, your experience may have been the same as that of thousands of travelers before you: you came back more tired than ever before. Your week at that so-called resort was worse than spending a week at your mother-in-law's. You were taken advantage of from the time you stepped off the plane and took that "discount" taxi to your hotel—for three times the normal price! And that hotel...$50 a day for a room that you hated, complete with food that you wouldn't eat if the restaurant bestowed it upon you gratis. You returned home with one goal in mind: to wring the neck of the travel agent who exiled you to such misery.

This book is an outgrowth of the experience of many travelers in this country. Right now, traveling is continuing to rise in cost, and shrink in value and at a rate which exceed any other part of the economy. There are hotel rooms in Puerto Rico which used to cost as little as $20 a day three years ago, and now cost $95! There are places in France where a family of four could spend $30 on a mediocre breakfast, and still leave hungry, anxiously awaiting lunch. In fact, travel has outstripped the general cost of living increases.

But travel does not have to be that way. Many of our friends and business acquaintances go on fabulous inexpensive vacations at least twice a year, not because they are smarter than the average person, but because through years of travel, they've picked up the inside secrets of travel. They know how to find the little pension in Barcelona or on the beach in Portugal where a room and full board is still less than $5 (yes, that's five) a night! This book will share those ideas with you.

Unfortunately, travel guides such as this have one serious limitation: They are able to give you basic principles with regard to travel; but travel is like a moving river which changes constantly. Therefore, the traveler who wishes to take advantage of current bargains must have constantly updated information. One source for this information is TRAVEL SMART, a monthly newsletter covering the "insider" aspects of the travel scene.

TRAVEL SMART is available by sending $19.00 for a one-year subscription to: TRAVEL SMART, Dobbs Ferry, New York 10522.

HAVE A GOOD TRIP!

II.

GETTING THERE

GETTING THERE BY AIRLINE. Recently I travelled to London. Sitting next to me in the first class cabin was a businessman who had spent $2000 round trip for that flight. He thought he had been lucky even to get on the flight in peak season.

Little did he know that in that same first class section was a woman who had paid $700 round trip. She was positive that her fare was the lowest rate permissible by law.

Neither of them could have imagined that I paid a mere $540 for that very same flight, round trip, just like theirs. In the same section of the plane, using the same first class china they used, and arriving at the same time at the same airport, but for $1460 less than he had paid, and for $160 less than the woman had paid. What's the point? Simple—today, the average person cannot afford to go to Europe or the Middle East, to South America or the Far East, cannot afford even to go to the other coast of this country, without obtaining a cut rate. For most, it's a charter flight to save dollars. Others investigate excursion flights, leisure class, super saver flights, apex fares, long range discounts, no frills, and even freebies.

The purpose of this section is to explain what airlines are all about, how their price structures work, and how to get yourself on a special flight to the dream vacation of your choice, at less than half the price others are paying! So, is it Rio or Paris? Read on!

CONFIDENTIAL AIRLINE INFORMATION. Most of the world's large scheduled airlines, like BOAC, Pan Am, or KLM, belong to a rate-fixing cartel called the International Airline Transportation Association (IATA) and are referred to as IATA Airlines in the travel industry. They all charge the same rates between any two destinations, and all allow interchange privileges—you may stop with no extra charge at any intermediate city at which any of these airlines makes a scheduled stop, (except on Apex excursion fares, or other specified pre-priced packaged fares and flights).

More than three-quarters of all IATA Airlines use modern jets, but a few (particularly in Central and South America) still fly turboprops. The turboprop airlines are allowed to charge lower fares because their flights usually take from one to two hours longer. Therefore, if you are not pressed for time, turbos can be a real savings.

On the other hand, there are many non-IATA Airlines which have not joined the cartel, and therefore, set their own rates, as they are in no way controlled by the governing board of the IATA.

One of the best known of these airlines is Icelandic, which has been in operation for more than twenty-five years, and has remained virtually accident free. It offers rates of $80-200 less than the IATA Airlines. In fact, the difference in price can be staggering—an IATA flight from London to

Singapore is nearly twice as expensive as a non-IATA flight via a certain smaller, friendlier, and more personal airline.

The IATA and non-IATA Airlines mentioned so far operate with regularly-scheduled flights. Planes take off whether full or three-quarters empty. There is a third group of airlines called the supplementals because they fly only when they have a planeload of passengers. Seats are sold by the planeload only.

It is important to realize that you have the upper hand! When you telephone an airline or go into a travel agent's office at random, often you are made to feel as though you are naive and/or a tightwad for asking for these lower-priced fares, and many times the travel agent will simply forget to tell you about them. But remember, all three types of airlines mentioned above are competing on the same routes, and consequently THEY ALL WANT YOUR BUSINESS. You have the upper hand in the situation, and it is up to you to acquire enough information to get cheap flights for yourself, because these flights are just sitting there waiting for you! Everywhere, the non-IATA Airlines are less expensive than the IATA, and the charter flights are cheaper than both. This rate comparison is well-known to smart travelers, and because of the significance in price differentials, the IATA lines have been forced to try various promotional group and excursion fares to remain competitive. Meanwhile to remain ahead, non-IATA lines and supplementals have similarly trimmed their rates. All this means two things:

1. Tremendous opportunities for smart travelers to save a lot of money by spending a few minutes shopping around for the right flight.

2. A "subject to change" airfare scene, including

the occasionally bankruptcy, as well as new airlines added to the list quite often.

Particularly today with the ever-changing gasoline situation, it is possible that some of the bargains we list will have been withdrawn, replaced, or increased by the date you sit down and read this book. Last month the petrol prices were skyrocketing and airlines were crying and warning the public about the impending ticket boosts. Yet, as I write this, the oil producing nations have just announced a glut of gasoline on the market, which will, in the next few months, be reflected in sudden lower, and unannounced previously, fares.

LOOPHOLES TO THE IATA. The IATA, like any other natural or man-made creature, has an "instinctive" urge to survive. Keeping this in mind, the IATA members long ago approved a series of regulations which permit any member to offer reduced rates for special groups if ordered to do so by its government. Needless to say, very few IATA lines have had any trouble convincing their governments to allow such special rates.

The most commonly-known special rates are the youth fares. Unfortunately, in many countries these youth fares have become history. Today, only Canadian and Mexican airlines offer these youth discounts, but at a huge 40 percent off, a flight from Montreal will still save you a load of money. In fact, anyone between the ages of 12-21 can save up to $300 by flying to Europe or the Middle East from Canada or Mexico. There are some restrictions, as many airlines require that you be away for a minimum (usually 21) and maximum (usually 45 or 60) number of days. However, the largest carrier at present utilizing this youth fare program offers such a fare from Canada to London with no minimum restriction and a maximum restriction of one year, and an off-season (after September 15) price of $560 round trip. You must make your reservation within five days of departure, so there is a certain amount of instability in this kind of travel. But you must realize too that the carriers who nowadays advertise these fares fly from not-so-popular points, and thus, do not usually fill their planes. My daughter has flown this method every year to her school in Europe and she has never once missed out on a reservation for the week that she wanted to leave. This sort of fare is designed for the college student, thus the maximum stay of one year, and consequently you cannot buy a one way ticket on this program.

One thing to note, is that if you cannot obtain a youth fare to your final destination, there are other possibilities about how to get to your destination. You can fly to whatever nearest point the airline runs, and then take a train (which in Europe are fun and civilized) or bus on to your dream city. Or, you can request the airline to arrange connections for you on to your city, and include such price in the student fare they are giving you. Many times this will still be just as low, or nearly, as if you had trained to the city. For example, to fly from Montreal to Rome on a youth fare, with all the above-mentioned allowances and restrictions, is priced round trip at $638! The youth fare-giving airline does not fly to Rome itself, but it makes the arrangements for you to connect on to that city on a regularly-scheduled airline and includes the price of the connecting flight in with your youth fare, thus giving you a youth fare, ostensibly, on two flights, one from Montreal to London and one from London to Rome. This savings, as compared to a regular flight, or even as compared to a standard standby fare coupled with a regular fare to connect you to Rome, is hundreds of dollars!

So if you live in the Northeast of the United States, it is well worth your while to take the train or bus to Toronto or Montreal, or any nearby Canadian city, and if you live in the southeast United States, do the same to Mexico City. Another advantage to youth fares, is that any American travel agent can handle your reservation for you, including arranging for the above-mentioned connections. Also, your ticket, once purchased, is usually good for one year.

Another "instinctive" life-saving effort made by the IATA is the excursion flight. These special rates are based on extended lengths of stay at your destination, usually 14-21 days, 22-45 days, or 150 days. Savings often go as high as 40 percent.

Hand in hand with the fight for life waged by IATA lines is the offering of special group rates at lower per-person costs on flights all over the world. These rates are particularly useful in countries which refuse to allow charters to land, and are also valuable as a savings for people who do not belong to organizations which offer charters.

Probably the cheapest way to fly, and the method I use ALWAYS, is the stand-by method. The disadvantage of this is immediately apparent: you do not know until the morning of departure whether or not you can leave that day, and you have to awake at five or six in the morning in order to go to the airport or ticket counter and get in line and find out if you will be allowed a seat. HOWEVER, it is the cheapest way to fly, you are given EXACTLY the same food and seating as the other economy passengers, you are given a choice of smoking or non-smoking sections, and you are afforded every other courtesy as the passengers who paid hundreds, literally hundreds of dollars more for their tickets than you did.

Each of the above is dealt with in detail in the following sections:

Savings I: Excursion flights. Excursion flights are designed to reduce your plane fare and thereby encourage you to spend more money in your destination's shops, markets, etc. The government benefits through taxes you pay on purchases in the foreign country; the airline benefits because it gets to charge a lower rate, making its fares more attractive, and encouraging the public to use them more often. There are two basic types:

1. Group Inclusive Tours (GIT's). These are actual tour packages designed to save you money on the cost of your flight, and which also include hotels, some meals, some touring, etc. These are extremely popular with the "businessman-vacationer" who will combine the low rates with some free sightseeing and business. The range of "guidedness" of these tours varies greatly, from merely the fare and hotel room and no other suggestions as to what to see or do, to the option of certain bus tours which would be prepaid and the price of which would be included in the main ticket.

The savings on these tours are tremendous. A hotel room at a high priced hotel in Guadalajara or Mexico City which normally is priced at 75 or 90 dollars, will be reduced as part of this package to 45 or 60 dollars. Notably, you can purchase New York (or any other gateway American city) to London and/or Paris, for one, two, three weeks, including hotel room and half-board, for a thousand dollars or under (higher the farther away from Europe is your starting point). Usually the savings on such a flight and stay amounts to fifty percent.

Of course there is always a catch on a savings of this kind. Full payment must be made within 15-45 days before departure, and a high cancellation fee (sometimes as much as twenty-five percent) will be levied if you change your mind. You must stay at the hotels which are booked for you by the tour, and you must see whichever London play they get tickets for, in order to receive the discount. In other words, these discounts are non-transferable, and if you don't like the hotel or the attractions, you must use them anyway or pay your own money to use others. If the minimum amount of passengers on such a group tour is not met, then there is a possibility that the tour will be cancelled. If your GIT is cancelled, you may switch to another, or get a full refund, but if your plans are not flexible, it IS possible that your vacation will be ruined. The cancellation of such a trip, to a common destinaton such as Madrid or London, is rare.

2. Advance Purchase Excursion Fares. (APEX). Generally, APEX offers up to fifty percent discounts on air flight fares. No package deals are offered in most cases: this is strictly an air fare deal. The savings are enormous, but there are certain disadvantages. No stopovers are permitted; there are stiff cancellation penalties, ranging from 10 to 15 percent; weekend flights have surcharges tacked on; and absolutely no changes are permitted in the schedule. Also, you must make the reservation at least three weeks in advance, and you must pay the full amount at that time.

3. Group Flights. There are many advantages to these flights, although recently more and more of them have been going out of business due to the lower fares offered by the airlines on the standard flights. It is anticipated that in the coming year, charters and other forms of group flights will become increasingly more popular, so the following information can be an investment in the future, although not immediately applicable in a great number of places.

Group flights are available through organizations, travel agents, airlines, clubs, etc., or you can sometimes join a pre-existing group flight which is looking to fill up empty spaces. With the advent of standby and APEX fares, as well as the Laker phenomenon, the charter flights have suffered enormously on the European front. Flights within Europe are still popular using this method, and flights to South and Central America are often available on a charter basis. But as for North America to Europe, these flights are, for the present, largely discontinued.

However, when the airlines are forced to raise fares for next year's trips, the following three classes of group fares will be helpful to know in order to avoid the scheduled flights and find yourself a good, cheap, charter flight:

1. **Travel Group Charters (TGC's).** This is the lowest, non-affinity charter rate available, and is created by travel agents who buy up forty or more seats on a flight and then sell these seats to their clients. Round trip TGC's are often less expensive than regularly scheduled, one-way flights. Passengers must deposit twenty-five percent of the fare when signing up, with the balance due within sixty days of departure. Obviously, this kind of flight is only good for people who can plan such a trip months in advance. A passenger may cancel out, but then the seat cannot be resold and the cost

of the cancellation is distributed among the remaining passengers, so your fare may go up by the time you pay the remaining amount. If the extra amount exceeds twenty percent, the entire flight will be cancelled and all money will be refunded. So, the savings are significant, but the insecurity of such a flight is also great.

Probably the greatest problem with this type of flight at this time, is that few exist except to Central America and the South Pacific. Flights to the most common destination for North Americans, under this program, at present are nearly impossible to find.

2. One-Stop Inclusive Tour Charters (OTC's). A few years ago the government ok'd the OTC, a program designed to cut airfares substantially and thereby placate the large American airlines which had complained bitterly about high American rates which were hurting business, especially when put up against European-based charters. However, the commercial American airlines have largely solved that problem, and the OTC's are mainly out of existence to Europe.

On an OTC, you fly with a group charter-style, but need not be a member of the chartering club or organization in order to join the flight. The savings, as with any charter-type flight, are great, but there are minimum length of stay requirements, as well as penalties for cancellation.

Unfortunately, as with TGC's, the available OTC is difficult to find. There are a couple still in operation to Central America and the Far East, but again, if you are on your way to a summer in Europe, a Christmas holiday in the Alps, or a Greek idyll, you simply will not find the OTC available to you.

3. Student Flights. Aside from the so-called youth fares or rates, there are hundreds of student flights offered every month, sponsored by travel groups at American universities and colleges. They generally cost fifty percent of the regular flight rate, and are not available to the general public, or even to a student who is not a student at the particular university which is offering the fare.

The only way to find out about them is through advertisements in student newspapers and in student unions. In the larger universities, the network universities such as University of California which has many, many campuses, there does exist a reciprocal agreement between campuses, so that if you are in school at UC Davis in north central California and your university travel center does not offer the flight to the destination or at the time that you want, you can choose from any of the flights at any of the campuses in the UC system. Also remember, extension class students (those who take one night class in a "fun" subject) and alumni are also eligible for these flights at many universities.

THE TRUE CHARTER AIRLINES. There are still several of these in operation, although they are not used nearly as widely as they were in the early and mid-seventies, before the commercial airlines instituted lower, regular fares.

It is still the case, though, that every year thousands of Americans utilize the "affinity" charters as a means of travelling at cut-rates. In this way, people pay much less than they would normally, and they travel with a group of people linked together through common membership in an organization or club. On the charter flight you receive all the same amenities that you would on the regular flight, many times more. The quality of food is excellent; the stewards and stewardesses are always courteous and give you personal service, even more so than the commercial airlines personnel who are often harried from too-closely scheduled flights. The baggage allowance on these affinity flights is frequently higher than a regular flight. And because the entire plane is filled with people in your group who are all going to the same place, you will not need to change planes or to make any special connection.

To organize a charter flight for your group, whether it be a special interest club, a church or an alumni association, first decide where you want to go, and then telephone one of the major airlines for help in deciding on a time, and a flight schedule. The international carriers often have special personnel available to do just this job, and they are all anxious to get your business as they are in competition with the supplemental carriers, the carriers set up specifically to fly charter groups. Ultimately, you will find that the supplemental carriers are cheapest, but first you can get all the help you need in planning from the special personnel at the international carrier offices. The following are two reputable supplemental carriers: World Airways, Inc., located at Newark International Airport in Newark, New Jersey, telephone from New York City—267-7111; and Capital Airways, 230 Park Avenue, New York, New York, telephone—212-883-0740.

It is important to realize that travel agents cannot book you onto these affinity charters unless you belong to the sponsoring organization, six months in advance, and neither can the airline company. If you are a non-member who desires space on an affinity flight, either join an organization or try to get a member to obtain space for you. My personal recommendation, however, is that charter flight rates these days are no lower than the new, standby and APEX fares advertised by regular airlines, and if you are not already a member of an organization, to join for this purpose, and to wait the six months, is unnecessary.

If you are organizing a trip for your club, the airlines can frequently help you make land arrangements as well as the flight arrangement, enabling you to offer your club or organization a rather impressive package. I am talking about significant savings. For example, the least expensive seat on a regularly scheduled airline from New York to Las Vegas is $200 more expensive than a well known charter group's latest price, which INCLUDED not only air fare but four days and three nights at a first class hotel! Another added bonus is that many charterers offer one free seat for every 15-20 you sell. Consequently, if you are the organizer, and you sell thirty seats, you and your spouse will fly and stay for free!

The disadvantages of course exist. The cancellation fee per person for these flights is extremely high, and there is the added possibility that the charter company, on the odd occasion, may cancel out on you. There will, of course be full refunds made if the company cancels on you, but the inconvenience of such an event is not worth the agony if it happens to your group.

MY PERSONAL RECOMMENDATION ON HOW TO FLY CHEAPEST:

Without a doubt, the cheapest, and most convenient for the price, way to fly ANYWHERE, is standby. Many scheduled airlines offer special fares on a standby basis in order to fill up the unsold seats. The fare is drastically reduced, and I have found it to be cheaper than any charter available, and cheaper than or at the very least comparable to, the APEX fares.

Each airline has different rules. You must go to the airport or the airline ticketing office in the major cities very early on the day you want to leave. You are issued a priority number in some cases and then you must return that day, a few hours before the time of departure of the flight, and you are issued your ticket and boarding pass. In other cases, the ticket is issued to you when you go to the airport the morning you want to leave. In that situation, you arrive at the airport one or two hours before flight time (the normal amount of time, which of course, varies with airline) and from then on you are treated as a regular customer. Usually the only time you need to stand in line is in the morning when you buy your ticket.

You are treated no differently than the other customers, you receive the same meals, arrive at the same time, etc. The only difference is that you stood in line for an hour or less early that morning and YOU PAID LESS THAN HALF THE REGULAR FARE!

Obviously, the main disadvantage to this kind of travel is that you never know if you are leaving until the day you actually try to travel. This sounds more unstable than it is, though. I have, for the past three years, travelled exclusively by this method, and I have NEVER been denied a seat. Never. I have saved thousands of dollars and have never been inconvenienced.

But remember one thing, in order to insure yourself a seat on the flight, find out what time the ticket office opens in the morning (usually seven or eight o'clock) and arrive an hour before that time.

MEET THE NON-IATA'S. I have singled out a few non-IATA airlines whose safety records, quality of service, and convenient departure sites make them most attractive. The listing is alphabetical, with no special preference in ordering.

Icelandic Airlines, 610 Fifth Avenue, New York, New York 10020. Offers jet flights from New York to Luxembourg, Iceland, and Scandinavia. The Luxembourg service is the lowest fare they have, and connections are made easily from Luxembourg to all points in Europe.

International Air Bahamas, Suite 737, Ingraham Building, 25 SE Second Avenue, Miami, Florida 33131. Offers savings on flights from Naussau to Luxembourg. Why not visit the Grand Bahamas for a few days, and then fly IAB to Europe? Another advantage is that IAB is an affiliate of Icelandic Airlines, so you might fly New York to Luxembourg, make your European stops, and then fly to Bermuda before boarding an IATA to come home.

Malaysian-Singaporian-Australian Travel Service (MSA), 10 Oxford Circus, London W1, England. Offers inexpensive flights from London to India and other Far Eastern lands via turboprop airlines owned by Arab states, or via 707's owned also by Arab states.

TRICKS OF THE TRADE. There are many other "tricks of the trade" open to smart travelers. Some of them may not be apparent at first glance, but that's part of the reason they have not been eliminated by the airlines—not many people take advantage of them. Others are really very logical, and would not be eliminated even if everyone started to use them.

I. Force the airline to absorb "extra costs". It is a well known fact that if you arrive late in Madrid and cannot fly on to Granada or Barcelona until the next afternoon, the airline should assume your overnight lodging and meal costs caused by their "failure" to provide a timely connection. The trick here is that if you study the air flight time-tables, it is relatively simple to find flights which will result in your getting "stuck" overnight or longer in a luxurious hotel in an interesting city and not having to pay a cent for the accommodation!

II. The cheap foreign fare. It's no secret that competition between airlines is a never-ending battle, with each airline looking to go one-up on its fellows. The result: in many foreign cities, particularly Bangkok; you can actually bargain with airline personnel to obtain lower rates. The key is to know which cities offer the best prices, and which are unreasonably expensive. The following countries DO NOT offer bargains and are the last places you should try to buy tickets in: Switzerland, Brazil, Columbia, Haiti, Panama, and many other South and Central American countries. The best bargains are obtained in India and Pakistan.

III. Ask around. Wherever you are looking to buy fare tickets from a destination to another destination, ask for the lowest possible price and ask at least three different airlines. Very often, a lazy or inexperienced clerk on one airline will fail to realize that there are alternatives to the standard "discount" rates, and not give you the cheapest possible price. Also, if you are flexible, tell the clerk you would be willing to fly on a different day if it meant extra savings.

IV. On stopover flights, purchase a ticket to the farthest point on your itinerary unless your agent proves that combination tickets will be cheaper in your case. For example, if you plan on going to Athens by way of London, it is usually much cheaper to buy a New York to Athens ticket than to buy a New York-London ticket and then buy a second London to Athens fare in the U.S.

V. Depart from the lowest-cost gateway city whenever possible. For example, if your destination is anywhere in Europe, fares are slightly cheaper from Boston than from New York, and they are at least seven percent cheaper from Montreal. From the Pacific Coast to Europe, the cheapest gateway cities are Vancouver and then Seattle.

VI. Never buy a separate fare from the west to the east, and then overseas. All transatlantic flights are rated from New York when the city of departure is to the west. The cost of a Denver to London flight includes that rate, as well as a fee covering the cost of a flight from Denver to New York. However, that flight from Denver to New York is at a discounted rate, substantially lower than the regular Denver-New York rate, so never buy a separate domestic air ticket to your gateway city.

Another important note is that Los Angeles and San Francisco have lower to-Europe flight rates than several more easterly-located western cities (i.e., Phoenix, Salt Lake City), so you would be better off bussing or driving "dead-head" to Los Angeles or San Francisco if you live in the central-western region of the United States, rather than flying directly from your city to Europe.

VII. Take advantage of European "Common Rated Cities". If you fly to the capital of most European countries, you can fly on FREE to a smaller city. Generally, you are not allowed a stopover in that capital city, but if you plan your flight so that no connection is available that night or day, you will have to have a day or so in the capital city also, at the expense of the airline!

VIII. Buy intra-European air flight tickets in Europe. This is an opportunity for tremendous savings. Let's say you travel by freighter to any European city, and then plan to fly to another location. If you purchase that air ticket in the U.S., you'll be paying up to seventy percent more than you would if you mae the purchase in Europe, because American travel agents can only sell normal economy class tickets for in-Europe flights. In Europe, you can purchase excursion and night flight tickets at substantial savings.

Another reason to wait until you reach Europe is that many European airlines offer special fifty percent discounts if you purchase your ticket no earlier than two p.m. of the day prior to departure and do not return before 1 p.m. the following Sunday.

The biggest European flight bargain of all is the Independent Tour Charter (ITC). These are 14-22 day vacations that include not only airfare, but room accommodations, meals and sightseeing at your destination. The savings are huge, and extend to non-European destinations upon occasion. There is nothing to join, and the only catch is that they can only be purchased in person, in Europe; but ITC operators are always willing to send their catalogs. Here are a few of the European ITC operators we've had success with:

Cosmos of London, 180 Vauxhall Bridge Road,
Westminster, London SW1 England.
Gastager Reisen, 8221 Inzell,

Postfach 1140, Germany.
Royaltours, 5 Kaasterweg, D-4000,
Dusseldorf, Germany.
Thomson Group, Greater London House,
Hampstead Road, London NW1 England.

IX. Always investigate the new low-rate offers. There has been a lot of talk about air train rates to Europe which can save you as much as fifty percent less than the current rates.

The basic trick on all of the above-listed fares and methods is to establish a plan of action for yourself—never accept the fare from one travel agent or from one airline ticket agent. Make a plan of people you will consult. Start at the airlines and check both with the non-IATA's and with a couple of the IATA Airlines for their lowest rates. Ask around at your union, your church, or any special interest group you belong to in order to find if they have charter flights or special deals to the place you want to go. When you think you have the lowest rate, contact the airline which serves the country you plan to visit and write to some ITC's for their rates. Then, when you have all the information, and not before you do, go to your travel agent and ask him/her if he/she can beat the price.

Bargains within the United States. As you've probably guessed, airlines are among the most heavily regulated and closely watched industries in the U.S. Surprisingly enough, they offer vast differences in prices for the same service. These price variations should be checked out by asking the airline a simple question: "Do you have excursion rates?"

Frequently airlines have these rates, but do not promote them because they come with limitations.

Yet, for the average traveler going on a vacation, these limitations are usually easy to live with. One major airline quoted did you comply with these very regulations without knowing about the special rate, and did you pay the higher fare? It is essential when planning any trans-U.S. vacation by air to ask this simple question: Do you have an excursion rate? It could save you hundreds of dollars.

Another money-saving tip is that it is more expensive to fly during the day, and it is most expensive to take a weekend day flight. You can save at least one hundred dollars on regular fares by flying during the week at night.

When making arrangements for your United States trip, be sure to check out the Super Saver fares and the standby fares, which reduce the cost of the ticket to well below a charter flight ticket price. And inquire about discounts for children, which can sometimes be as high as fifty percent off the regular ticket price.

Be sure to check out the smaller airlines, too. There are dozens of regional airlines across the United States which offer incredible savings on packages, in order to compete with the larger companies. It is always a good idea to check these out before being ticketed on a major line, because an airline such as Ozark or Allegheny will offer you a trip to your destination PLUS stopovers or triangle-type fares or group fares (where the group can be as small as the four people in your family), all for the same price as the large company's regular ticket from one city to another with no extras.

When you are investigating these savings, never take your travel agent's word for it. In many cases these so-called experts in travel are nothing more than telephone answering services and ticket writers. They have been taught to fill in a form, but that's all. The overwhelming majority have never even been more than one hundred miles from their home cities and are often "unaware" of specials because they are paid by commission.

THE BIG BOUNCE! Airlines are a major business, and like most businesses, they always seek to make the largest profit possible. So, before you fly you should be well aware of one cruel fact of the airlines: they can and will bounce you if they've overbooked your flight. What does this mean? One way airlines try to increase their profits is to overbook flights. They know that, on most flights, slightly more than five percent of those with reservations do NOT show up, so they usually sell a few more tickets than there are actually seats for.

Airlines got away with this for years. People would come to the airport, their flight would be full, and it would be nothing more than tough luck, with no recourse for the passenger—they were "bounced" off their flight.

Then, one day an airline did this to consumer advocate Ralph Nader. He didn't like it at all, especially because he missed a paid speaking engagement because of the bounce. Mr. Nader took that airline to court and won a Supreme Court case, leaving the airlines in a rather uncomfortable position of being legally responsible and liable for damages to anyone they bounced.

Of course, the airlines were not about to give up the great business opportunity overbooking and bouncing provided, so they cried to the Civil Aeronautics Board. The CAB, in its infinite wisdom, realized that the Supreme Court decision was indeed the law of the land, and knew that it had to come up with a solution which would protect the consumer enough to please the courts, and protect the airlines enough so their profits could stay where they were.

The solution: a new regulation governing bounces. Now, if you get bounced, the airline must get you to your destination within four hours of your scheduled departure time or incur a penalty. The penalty is a fine of no less than $25, but no more than $200, payable to you, the bouncee, plus free passage on the next available flight. This is in addition to a complete refund of your ticket price, and must be completed within twenty-four hours. If the airline fails to comply with this within the twenty-four hour prescribed period, you have ninety days to file a claim.

The moral of the story is this: if you get bounced don't storm off muttering angry words about bringing a lawsuit. Stay right there, demand a copy of the CAB regulations on bouncing and the necessary forms you must file to get your money back, free passage, and penalty fee. In almost every case, if you display defiance and a knowledge of the bounce rules, airline officials will suddenly become very congenial to you, and will offer you a wide variety of odds and ends to calm you down.

If you do get bumped, and you get no immediate satisfaction, or if you have any questions about American airline regulations (and regulations of foreign airlines operating from American airports) write to the Office of Consumer Affairs, Civil Aeronautics Board, Washington, D.C. 20428. They also offer a variety of informative booklets and pamphlets on consumer rights vis-a-vis airlines.

The letter you send may well result in a free flight plus some spending money!

GETTING THERE BY SHIP. The luxury liner fleets of the United States, Great Britain, and France have dwindled away into nothing, but replacing them are growing numbers of Greek, Russian, Italian, Scandinavian, and Yugoslavian passenger liners. In many cases, you will be traveling a renamed, refurbished Cunard Liner, complete with old-fashioned first-rate service and comfort.

Although steamships are not the bargains they once were, there are still many inexpensive lines with superior service. Furthermore, another smart discount, which is little-known, is to combine a sea voyage with an air flight—most of the steamship companies have special five to ten percent discounts on fares if you "pair up" your means of transportation. Discounts are also offered on cross-Atlantic voyages used as gateways to trips around the world. Many steamers also allow you to disembark for extended periods of time at ports of call along the way, at no extra charge—you simply board the next liner that comes through, usually in less than ten days.

To ship out on a luxury liner, you must contact a travel agent that handles steamship companies. There are hundreds of these, and they are listed as such, steamship agents, in the yellow pages of your local directory. Below I have gathered together a list of certain luxury liner services in existence at the time of this writing (although some may have folded by the time you read this book because of continued pressure from the airlines):

> Chandris Cruises
> Costa Line
> Cunard Line (still in existence)
> Holland American Line
> Italian Line

K Lines Hellenic Cruises
March Steamships
Norwegian American Line
Royal Viking Line

As I noted above, you must go through a travel agent to obtain schedules, rates, etc.

Travelling by Tramp Steamer (freighter). If you've considered tramp-steamer (freighter) travel as a transportation bargain, you should be careful. True, freighters provide excellent rates for overseas travel, and an excellent vacation for people who want to be off on their own (writers, artists, etc.). However, as a form of transportation to a vacation land, they can be a mistake for many.

Tramp-steamers offer several advantages. First, they offer plenty of time to read, write, listen to records, see the whole ship from stem to stern, and even help to sail it, if you desire. Second, the cabins are generally as good as, and often superior to, those on liners, with excellent food on most freighters (particularly Dutch and Norwegian), and an outside location for good viewing. You can bring your own bar aboard, so you need not worry about missing your favorite drinks, and you are allowed to bring several hundred pounds of luggage at no extra charge.

However, freighter travel offers one distinct disadvantage and several possible ones. The obvious negative factor is that sailing and arrival dates are never firm; neither are locations. Many times, a freighter scheduled to land in one pot may have its cargo sold while at sea, and be diverted a thousand miles to the new owner's warehouse. When that happens you have no choice but to go to the new destination.

Another problem is that there are few, if any,

forms of planned entertainment. Yes, there will be an occasional movie or sing-along, but there won't be any gala balls, or talent shows, or miniature golf courses. Furthermore, because there will be less than sixteen passengers in almost all cases (prescribed by international law—to carry more, the freighter must have a doctor on board), you have to be prepared to make your own fun (especially if you do not get along with the other travellers).

Freighters are somewhat sexist in their regulations. Pregnant women are now allowed on any tramp-steamers, and women in general are occasionally unwelcome guests because of superstitions about women aboard ships. This is rare, though.

If you are over sixty-five years of age, you must obtain a doctor's certificate of good health endorsing the voyage.

If a scheduled run is twenty-five days, and bad weather forces an extension to twenty-eight, you are not charged for the extra days aboard ship...but your plans may be ruined, or your vacations shortened. By the way, trips range from ten to more than one hundred days, depending on length of voyage. Rates are based on the number of scheduled days at sea.

In determining whether or not a tramp-steamer is for you, consider the following:

1. *Are your plans flexible?* If not, don't go by steamer because times and places are often changed at sea...and go where the freighter goes, like it or not.

2. *Plan early.* A genuine tramp-steamer cannot carry more than twelve (sixteen if coastal travel only) passengers unless it provides a doctor, more staff members, and additional life-saving gear. Also,

because of the popularity and small space, you will probably have to wait from three months to two years to get a berth.

3. *What do I take?* Leave your fine dresses and tuxedo at home. Instead, stock leisure and sporty dress items. Bring your own laundry detergent— most freighters have washers, dryers, etc., but do not supply detergent. Don't forget suntan lotion, raincoat, binoculars, map, sewing kit, books to read, and can and bottle openers. The liquor is duty-free, so take advantage of it.

4. *Learn about the ship you are considering.* Is it air conditioned? Where are the guest cabins located? What kinds of accommodations are available? Are televisions, radios, and stereos available for your use?

5. *Learn about the ports of call and shore excursion schedule.* Be sure to carry a small phrase book for unfamiliar languages. A big advantage to freighter travel is that going ashore is not accompanied by five hundred to two thousand tourists, and prices do not skyrocket when you arrive.

6. *Food.* Be prepared for a really nice surprise because it is rarely less than excellent. Here is a typical menu from a regular U.S. to Europe line:

Breakfast. Eggs to order, sausages, assorted dry cereals, potatoes, toast, hot cakes with syrup, coffee, tea, milk.

Lunch. Chicken delight, two to three hot vegetables, fruit pie, beverages.

Dinner. Salad, soup, appetizer, roast prime ribs of beef, two to three hot vegetables, cakes and fruits, beverages.

Foreign freighters are always well-stocked in the

liquor department and Western European and U.S. lines are also loaded with sweets for snacks.

Be prepared to eat a little earlier than you may be used to: Breakfast is from 7:30 a.m. to 9:00 a.m., lunch from 11:30 a.m. to 12:30 p.m., and dinner is served from 5:00 p.m. to 6:30 p.m.

You can expect fine dining, especially because you will be eating along with the captain and the officers of the ship, and the food will also be plentiful. In fact, most people we know who've had their share of luxury liners and luxury cruises agree that freighter food is the best afloat...and with good reason. The chef is only cooking for forty to eighty people, instead of five hundred or more.

7. *Get to know the crew members.* They are usually among the most interesting and well-travelled people you'll ever meet. They will undoubtedly desire to share all of their experiences with you, and will also tell you where to go when you go ashore.

8. *Fares.* These range upwards from fifty dollars a day. The longer the trip, the less expensive the per diem assessment. For example, freighter fare from the U.S. to Italy can be half the fare to and from the same destinations on the luxury liner, and by the time you get around to paying for the extras on the liner, you'll have spent a lot more. By contrast, the freighter offers a much cheaper overall transportation cost, with even fewer hidden extras.

9. *Tipping.* Do not overtip. Five percent of the fare is a just amount, and should be distributed on the last day of the voyage, or weekly if it's a long trip. Remember, tipping is not an accepted custom on the ships of some countries, notably, Japanese, Russian, and Chinese ships.

10. *Obey the rules of the ship.* They are designed

for your comfort and safety. Don't fill the captain's ears with trivial complaints. Don't be late for meals, throw trash overboard in ports, leave doors unlocked, enter areas which are restricted (unless you have permission), and do not go on the ship's bridge without the permission (and preferably invitation) of the ship's captain or mate.

The following is a list of tramp-steamer (freighter) specialists in the United States and Canada:

Traveltips
40-21 Bell Boulevard
Bayside, New York

DuPont Plaza Travel Service
300 South Biscayne Boulevard Way
Miami, Florida

Air and Marine Travel Service
Box F
501 Madison Avenue
New York, New York

Commonwealth Travel Service, Inc.
Dillingham Avenue
Falmouth, Massachusetts

Freighter Cruise Service
5925 Monkland Avenue
Suite 103
Montreal, Quebec, Canada

World Wide Travel Service
300 Wilson Avenue
Downsview, Ontario, Canada

AAA Worldwide Travel Service
3525 Northwest 23rd Street
Oklahoma City, Oklahoma

Cruises Exclusively, Inc.
Suite 917
Wrigley Building
400 North Michigan Avenue
Chicago, Illinois

World Wide Travel Bureau, Inc.
1408 Industrial Building
Detroit, Michigan

Cosmopolitan Travel Company
550 South Vermont
Suit 1201
Los Angeles, California

Norman Read Travel Service
1480 Marine Drive
West Vancouver, B.C.

Travelwide International
1166 Seventh Avenue
San Diego, California

Mathis Travel
22 Battery Street
San Francisco, California

Pickard Travel Service
3015 East Thomas Road
Phoenix, Arizona

Holiday Travel
1826 Northeast 40th Avenue
Portland, Oregon

Here is a list of actual freighter companies we have
taken passage with. All are more than satisfactory:

Alcoa Line
1 World Trade Center
New York, New York

American President Lines
601 California Street
San Francisco, California

Argentine Lines
1 World Trade Center
New York, New York

W. Bruns & Company
Postfach 100809
2 Hamburg 1, West Germany

Holland America Line
2 Pennsylvania Plaza
New York, New York

Knutsen Line
Bakke Steamship Company
650 California Street
San Francisco, California

Lauro Lines
Lauro Building
Via Cristoforo Colombo
45 Naples, Italy

Orient Overseas Line
510 Montgomery Street
San Francisco, California

Polish Ocean Lines
Gdynia American Line Inc.
1 World Trade Center
New York, New York

CRUISE SHIPS. The ultimate vacation escape for many is the cruise. Just pampered luxury for you. Six great meals a day...a stroll around the deck...starlight dancing. It's truly the best way to really unwind.

Interestingly enough, no other form of travel has such wide differences in prices. For example, every day you'll see ads in the major papers reading "from $500 to $1509". And all on the same ship! What does it mean? Simply, it means that two of you will save hundreds of dollars if you take the less expensive room...and, surprisingly enough, the difference in accommodations is not as great as you might imagine. This is especially true if you take the best of the budget cabins...which, of course, go first.

What all this means is: make your reservations EARLY. Write to the steamship lines and ask for sailing dates. Then, make your reservations immediately. Sometimes, this means six months or a year in advance. Fortunately, you can usually get a refund up to six weeks prior to the scheduled departure.

Look at it this way, you'll be travelling to Europe or the Caribbean with people who paid twice as much as you did for the same cruise...and laugh your way to the bank with the money you save!

For those who are unfamiliar with cruises, here is

a list of typical cruise activities below:

Captain's Champagne party
Singles Cocktail party
Piano concert
Jousting contest
Masquerade
Caribbean night
Casino night
Talent night
Humorous deck games
Crew show
Bridge, canasta, rummy
Dance classes and contests
Swimming
Movies
Shuffleboard
Diving
Deck tennis
Trap shooting
Bingo
Table tennis
Snorkling
Skin Diving
Late night buffets
Continental Revue

GETTING THERE BY TRAIN. Getting around your vacation destination will be covered in the next section, including train travel in European and South American countries; however, if you are making a journey to a destination in the continental United States, you might think about taking Amtrak, rather than flying. Generally, there are two reasons for taking the trains of the world: low cost and convenient travel; or you might use them for that best of all reasons: good old nostalgia. In the United States, the reasons people take trains is a mixture of both, but as our railroads continue to decay, the nostalgia theme is ever-increasing, plus the fact that it's often just as cheap to go by streamline bus.

Amtrak is under never-ending criticism for unclean cars, poor service, unreliable departure-arrival, and general inconveniences. Most of the system is useful as a scenic route, largely because the tracks and railbeds have decayed to the point where speed limits go as low as ten miles per hour.

However, there are several excellent exceptions, especially the Boston-New York-Washington, D.C. Metroliners, which offer fast, efficient, economical transportation at a competitive price (less than $50).

Amtrak also offers a new family plan which can give up to a twenty-five percent discount for spouse and children travelling with a full-fare adult in certain areas. There are certain limitations as to when such travel can be made utilizing this discount fare.

For actual tours of the U.S., contact: American Rail Tours, Michigan Avenue, Chicago, Illinois, or Amtour Corporation, 421 Powell Street, San Francisco, California.

One of the most enchanting aspects of American rail travel is the historical element. A family travelling by train across the United States is given the unique chance of "pioneering" again. Tours can be mapped out wherein you retrace the routes of the covered wagons, or of any particular explorer/pioneer figure in American history who captures your fancy. Did you ever long to be Daniel Boone, or Merriweather Lewis? Follow their trail by taking the train along the routes they mapped hundreds of years ago. This kind of trip can be extremely educational and fun, and is much more interesting, and no more expensive a way of getting from your home town to your vacation destination as the airline companies.

A sharp contrast to the United States' lackluster rail service can be seen in our northern neighbor's government-subsidized, seldom crowded, fine train service. High-speed trains travel coast to coast through splendid, majestic scenery.

Canadian National Railways offers the "Super Continental," a full-service, coast to coast ride, complete with day-nighter cars, cross-over coaches, and sleepers. You can even arrange to ship your car ahead, or combine the train ride with car rentals throughout the Canadian Rockies. Discounts for families, groups and senior citizens are the rule, rather than the exception.

Canadian-Pacific Railways offers a special service in a skyline coach with reclining seats, reservations at no extra cost, special tourer-domed cars to let you take in all of the scenery, fine dining, and sleeping facilities unmatched in the Western Hemisphere.

GETTING THERE BY BUS. The major bus companies offer various types of see-America passes good for unlimited travel for certain periods of time. For those who do not mind travelling on standard, air-conditioned, one rest room buses, they are a good deal. Often in the off-season, the larger national bus companies will offer a special one-way fare, whereby you are allowed to travel as far as you want in one direction for a flat fee.

There is also an alternative cross-America bus plan which is becoming more and more popular— the day leisure trip. Simply put, the buses travel scenic routes designed for good view, and stop no later than 6:00 p.m. for overnight accommodations at inexpensive small hotels and motels. Prices are very reasonable, and when you can convince a whole bus to visit a specific landmark or site, you'll get discount admissions.

A third means of bus travel which continues to grow, albeit, somewhat surreptitiously, are the so-called underground mattress bus lines. These are usually operated by young people who register their mini-buses as "church owned" vehicles to avoid Interstate Commerce Commission hassles and taxes levied by the government. They are not allowed to advertise because of their "church-owned" status, so you must contact them through a referral service known as Travelers Exchange Unlimited, or other local names. They are hard to find unless you are in the know. One way to quickly get in touch with these companies, is to contact the travel service at your local university. These student operated services always have information about the cheapest ways to travel, and certainly this type of bus travel is one of the least expensive. The drawback with it, of course, is a certain level of unreliability. The bus may break down, it may not arrive on time, or it may leave late. The accommodations are terribly uncomfortable, i.e., there are usually no seats on the bus, but rather, mattresses on the floor where you sit and sleep, if it is an overnight journey. However, the savings are great, as these buses are far cheaper than the regular lines, and as little as one sixth the cost of a comparable air fare ticket.

Another bus transport bargain is the charter bus, especially popular for jaunts to the ballgame, or one-shot streaks down to resorts. These sell well on college campuses, where students grab low-cost, one week vacation opportunities.

INSURANCE FOR YOUR VACATION: A MUST. When travelling, the cost of a floater insurance policy is miniscule, and the protection it gives is worth one hundred times the price.

Your insurance agent can be most helpful in this area. For example, a twenty-five thousand dollar life and accident insurance policy with a twenty-five hundred dollar theft policy is the low cost of ten or fifteen dollars a week. Remember, too, that the theft of your camera might add fifty percent to the cost of your trip. Protecting it in advance costs a few pennies. Do not be lulled into blind trust of the airline baggage insurance policies mentioned on your ticket. Many thefts occur in airports (and you are not covered after you pick up your baggage), as well as in hotels and restaurants. Also, many airlines attempt to waive their liability above a certain limit; the legality of this waiver attempt is questionable, and courts have gone either way.

As far as auto insurance is concerned, beware: Mexico does not honor United States auto insurance. You can obtain a Mexican policy reasonably through your agent, or when you cross the border.

Another insurance value is from the National Travel Club (Travel Building, Floral Park, New York) which offers thousands of dollars worth of insurance for roughly ten dollars. Contact them for full details.

If you plan to ride on a charter flight, you might also want to get some insurance against the flight's cancellation. If you are organizing a charter flight, you had better get some insurance against cancellation to protect yourself from a big business loss, and possible suits.

Another kind of insurance is health insurance specifically for your trip. There are many types available, some to refund you the money for your trip if you get sick abroad, some to pay for your untimely return home in such a case, and some to pay for any hospital stay or doctor's care you require abroad. This is always a good idea, as it is the worst thing in the world to be sick in a foreign country and worry about the details of medical attention payment (which can be quite costly) or how to get home before your charter flight returns.

As you well know, insurance rates vary from state to state, so protect yourself accordingly.

KNOW YOUR TRAVEL AGENT. How many times have you chosen a travel agent at random and ended up with a package tour that left you stranded at the airport with half the package of your tour missing and no one to deal with directly? I remember once going to a brand new travel agent on the vague recommendation of a friend of mine, planning a trip to Mexico, and walking out of the travel agent's office with my tickets and airport transfers and hotel reservations in the agent's neat little envelope. I was so impressed with the agent's efficiency. Upon arrival in Guadalara, however, there was no one to meet me, I had to pay a huge amount, cash, to get to the hotel from the airport, and once at the hotel I found the reservations had not been made. Selecting a travel agent is as important as selecting the right color television. They all look great on the outside, they all seem efficient, because they are primed for display. It's when you take it home and plug it in, or when you sign up for a vacation and get to your destination, that you know what you really have.

A good travel agent can be valuable, and their

services cost you nothing. A travel agent is paid a commission from airlines, hotels, restaurants, etc. But that commission is often less than ten percent. You must realize that above all else, your agent is also a business person whose profit depends on routing you as quickly as possible onto a satisfactory trip with a minimum of hassles. After all, the agent relies on long-term customers; they want you to keep coming back every time you want to plan a vacation.

Most agents specialize in all-inclusive, minimum-complexity for the tour packages. But you, as a smart traveller, prefer to pick your own transportation, hotels, landmarks, etc. You enjoy doing your own preliminary planning, and have no qualms about sending away for information literature and building your own programs. How should you select your agent? Here are a few hints:

1. Visit at least two or three. Try to ascertain how down to earth each one is. Is he/she offering a plan created for you, or just trying to sell you a plastic package deal?

2. Determine the extent to which they try to understand you. It's always a good idea to just sit down and chat about sports, the car, or whatever is on your mind. If the agent is amiable and worldly in their knowledge, chances are you've made a good start. If the agent seems overly interested in jumping into a contract for a trip to wherever, just say thanks and leave. Does the agent tell you about trips he/she has taken to the destination you have chosen? This is always a good sign: that of personal experience and the willingness to tell you the inside, human interest story on their own vacations. You'll save yourself innumerable future headaches, if you choose a travel agent who has the time and the knowledge to

share with you.

3. Does the agent reflect on and consider your ideas, or does he/she immediately steer you to another location?

4. Are you affiliated with a large organization? If so, use the same agent the organization does. It will help you get more personalized service if you drop the organization name around, especially if the organization is a large account.

5. Use a large agency if you can get them to really work for you. They have more bargaining power when dealing with hotels and airlines than smaller agencies do, and they can often get you space in that Ft. Lauderdale hotel on December 20th, something the smaller agency would find impossible. The only real advantage to a small agency is in the availability of personal attention. But your real interest in the agent has to be what you get on your vacation, and not whether or not you are spoon-fed caviar in their office.

6. Bounce your itinerary off the agent and get the agent's reaction. This way, you show the agent you know something about the vacation you are planning, and your extra degree of preparation may well stimulate the agent's interest. Ask the agent for any ideas or insight he/she may have regarding your plans.

In the end, you'll probably start with an agent who has attracted you through low prices or friendship; after one or two vacations planned with this agent, you'll know whether or not that agent can really deliver. If you're satisfied, do not change. Keep using the same agent again and again—the longer you use the same business, the better the prices usually become, and the more likely you'll get cooperation when that emergency comes.

If you are dissatisfied with your agent, tell them why and explain that you plan to look elsewhere. If the agent is serious about his/her business, you'll get satisfaction; if not, you'll be glad you switched.

III.

GETTING AROUND AFTER YOU ARRIVE

The world of public mass transportation which surrounds the United States is a sharp contrast to that which we see here at home. Ask any New Yorker about commuting on the Long Island Railroad, and he'd probably rather die than use it. Ask a Chicagoan about using the city's buses and elevated trains, and she'll laugh in your face. And of all the insane things to do, who would ever take a train from San Francisco to Seattle!

But in other countries, particularly European nations, Australia, Japan, the USSR, and China, public mass transportation is inexpensive, fast, comfortable, and a real traveller's bargain. European rail service is among the finest in the world. Streamlined trolley cars operate in many of the world's finest tourist-attraction cities. Buses are usually comfortable, and separate express lines take the stop-and-go aspect out of this type of transit.

Why is mass transportation better overseas? Probably because most foreigners simply cannot afford to buy and maintain automobiles of their own, and are not used to an automotive society.

Their governments are well aware of this, and must maintain solid mass transit as the alternative. If you know any Italians, you've probably heard them say that "at least Mussolini made the trains run on time"—and that's something of ultimate importance to people in most other countries.

So what does this all mean? As much as you are used to having your private car at your own disposal twenty-four hours a day, when you are abroad, use the mass transit opportunities which present themselves. Take a train from Brussels to Paris or Amsterdam—it's a lot cheaper than a quick flight, and with an average speed of eighty miles an hour, almost as fast. Don't take a taxi from the airport when in most cases the public buses are less than one-half the price (see the airport transfer chart included herein).

You can save more than fifteen dollars a day by using public transportation in most other countries, and that's not peanuts on a month-long tour!

Because most of you will fly to your holiday destination, and then need to take some mode of transportation from the airport to your hotel, I am including a special chart to give you some idea of the prices of public transportation transfers from airport to city centers. Of course, these prices are flexible, particularly with the state of the dollar against other currencies, so please be sure to account for the change in prices when you figure these amounts into your trip budget.

Country	City	Miles from Airport	($) Average Coach to City
Austria	Vienna	10	2.60
	Graz	6	2.60
	Linz	5	2.60

Country	City	Miles from Airport	($) Average Coach to City
Australia	Canberra	4	2.00
	Sydney	7	1.75
	Melbourne	14	3.20
	Hobart	40	4.00
	Adelaide	3	2.00
	Brisbane	4	2.60
	Perth	6	2.75
Belgium	Brussels	10	3.75
Denmark			
	Aarhus	20	5.50
	Odense	10	3.50
Finland	Helsinki	12	2.50
	Tampere	3	1.50
France	Paris—CDG	16	5.50
	Orly	13	2.50
	LeBourget	8	2.50
	Nice	4	1.50
West Germany	Berlin	6	4.00
	Cologne	12	3.50
	Dusseldorf	4	3.20
	Frankfurt	8	3.80
	Hamburg	8	3.75
Great Britain	London-Heathrow	15	3.00
	Gatwick	30	5.00
	Glasgow	45	5.75
	Manchester	10	2.10
Greece	Athens	6	1.50
Israel	Tel Aviv	11	1.00

Country	City	Miles from Airport	($) Average Coach to City
Italy	Rome	17	3.00
	Milan	29	3.00
	Turin	10	2.50
	Venice	8	1.75
Japan	Tokyo	10	5.10
	Osaka	9	1.25
Mexico	Mexico City	8	2.90
	Acapulco	6	4.90
Norway	Oslo	6	3.75
	Bergen	12	4.00
Portugal	Lisbon	3	.50
Spain	Madrid	5	.75
	Barcelona	5	.75
	Malaga	15	1.25
	Majorca	6	1.20
Sweden	Stockholm	23	5.50
Switzerland	Geneva	4	3.20
	Zurich	7	5.60
Yugoslavia	Belgrade	12	1.20
	Dubrovnik	13	1.20

As compared to these prices, the cost of an entire cab from the airport the above-specified distances to the city centers can be anywhere from three times the above amounts to ten times the above amounts. And this does not include the extras added on in taxis for transportation of baggage, for extra parties, and for the tip that you will give the driver, which is always a substantially larger tip when much baggage is being driven to a hotel. As you can see, using the mass public transportation in this case will save you many dollars.

TRAINS IN EUROPE. There are more than one hundred thousand miles of railroad tracks in Europe, and the tracks and trains are well-maintained and clean. To introduce non-Europeans to their fine service, the European railroads sell passes good on evry railroad in thirteen countries, called a EURAILPASS. This is without a doubt the cheapest means of transportation, as well as the most comfortable and reliable, if you plan to cover a lot of ground on your European tour. You can only buy this sort of pass here in the United States. It is good for *unlimited travel* all across Europe, and includes free passage on certain ferries. The prices change each summer and as of this writing the new prices have not yet gone into effect. You can buy a pass for different lengths of time from two weeks to three months. They are first class passage on the trains, and cost anywhere from two hundred and fifty dollars upward. The value is more than worth it, though, as a ticket on a train from Paris to Munich, for example, will cost approximately sixty dollars, a return fare will be one hundred and twenty. If you make two or three such trips you will have already have paid for your Eurailpass.

You can purchase these passes at any travel agent in this country or at the tourist offices of any European country. Remember, though, that they may only be bought in the United States and that once your name is on them they are not transferrable. They are activated by the stamp the conductor places on the pass upon first use, and are good from that time to the extent of the type of pass you have bought.

If you plan to stay within one country, every national railroad offers its own special plans and discounts. If you are travelling any substantial distance (fifty miles or more) go first class...second class is exactly that! Also, remember that the above Eurailpass is not good in Great Britain, which has its own special pass discussed below.

Scanning the national railways.

Austria. The fourteen day, unlimited travel pass, which is also available for seven days and one month.

Belgium. A reduced fare plan which includes all rail and bus transportation. This includes tourist discounts at landmarks, restaurants, etc.

Denmark. Rail and bus discount pass, and free use for ten days with a special pass.

France. Features many different kinds of discounts via a card which you must purchase. This card is good for thirty days, and offers twenty percent discounts.

West Germany. A twelve and one half percent discount on all trips covering more than two hundred kilometers (less than one hundred and twenty miles).

Great Britain. British pass offers free travel on railroads and several ferries and steamers for seven to thirty days. This pass must be bought outside the country.

Ireland. Offers the Rambler ticket, good for free use for fifteen days. With a special added fee, you will have free use of all buses, too.

Italy. Features an unlimited travel pass which must be bought outside the country on a per day fee; also offers special family discounts.

The Netherlands. Offers an eight day ticket for a small fee. This is a particularly peculiar deal, in that this is only valid if you travel more than four hundred eighty kilometers in that period (two hundred eighty-five miles).

Norway. Groups of ten travellers get twenty-five percent off.

Portugal. Discount tickets sold on. basis. of distance. The minimum distance is fifteen hundred kilometers (eight hundred eighty-five miles). This ticket is good for three months for a cheap fare. Also offered are limited round-trip tickets at a thirty percent discount.

Spain. Discount based on minimum of three thousand kilometers (seventeen hundred sixty-six miles). The savings here is about twenty-five percent.

Switzerland. Offers special Holiday Pass for non-residents, available outside the country only. Valid on government-operated trains, buses, boats, and allows a fifty percent discount.

Africa. Rail transportation is a good idea in South Africa, where old-fashioned steam locomotives offer a spectacular scenic ride as part of sixteen-day tours. Otherwise, avoid all African railroads like you would tsetse fly.

Australia. Offers a great Austrailpass which must be purchased outside the country. Travel on a system of track that is over twenty-seven THOUSAND miles long for fourteen days. Extensions of seven days are available in Australia for a small fee; monthly rates are also available.

New Zealand. Free rail use for fourteen days for one flat fee.

Far East. Japan is good, with special discounts; otherwise, trains are expensive, crowded and unreliable.

South and Central American countries. Do not

take the trains. They are cheap but completely unreliable. Instead, rent a car or hire a taxi for a long journey. The rates of taxis in these countries are cheap, too.

Middle East. Definitely the place to hire a car. Do NOT take trains in the Middle East.

USSR. When you tour the Soviet Union, you will always tour with a group, so you will have no choice about which trains you will take or whether you will take trains at all. As a rule, tourist groups in the Soviet Union fly from city to city rather than taking the train, and just as well; airlines in Russia are much more reliable than the train system.

A FEW WORDS ABOUT GETTING FROM PARIS TO LONDON. Because most people planning a European trip for the first time land in London and travel on to the continent, notably to Paris, it seems essential to point out that a wide variety of rates and methods of transportation are available for such journeys. The flight, certainly, from Heathrow to Paris is the quickest way to arrive. However, couple with the high price of the ticket (about fifty dollars at the time of this writing) the airport transfer fees at both ends, the taxis to and from the points of airport limousine service within the city, and the price is even higher than you would anticipate. Certainly it takes a mere hour to fly from one city to the other, but the transfer time, the waiting time, and the traffic time must all be figured in to your calculation of which is most convenient, quickest, and cheapest.

I would, for my money and for travellers not in a hurry, always recommended the many varieties of train, ferry combinations. A weekend round trip rate from London to Paris can be as low as forty dollars return. The one way, night boat train to

Paris is approximately forty dollars one way, with of course, no restrictions on returning. A day journey would cost about fifty dollars.

The varieties of travel are endless. Most people choose the train-ferry-train from London to Dover to Calais to Paris. But there is also the train-Hovercraft-train (Seaspeed), which cuts the time by a few hours, because the Hovercraft crosses the channel in little over an hour, smoothly and in a plane atmosphere gliding above the water. To cut the cost of the crossing, many people prefer to take the coach (bus) from London to Dover instead of the train. These packages can cut the price about ten to fifteen dollars.

My favorite method of crossing is the Hydrofoil, a new addition to the variety. This small, but quite comfortable and VERY SMOOTH boat, leaves right from the dock at the Thames near Tower Hill, inside the city of London, thus eliminating one leg of the old-fashioned journey. It takes you directly across the channel to Ostende or Dieppe, where you make a prearranged train connection to either Amsterdam or Paris or Brussels if you wish. The time is cut by many hours and the price is about the same. The ride is quite a bit more comfortable.

PLANES IN EUROPE. Europeans are a continent of vacationing people. They holiday in the summer, but also in the winter and fall. Consequently, the place to obtain cheap, adequate and reliable vacation flights from one destination on the European continent to another, is right within Europe itself. And I know of no better place than London. The English are great travellers and hagglers about their package tours. In order to find the cheapest flights possible in London to points on the continent, you can, of course, try travel agents at no charge. Also effective is to buy a magazine called "Time Out" which lists, in the back, dozens of agencies and cheap means of travel, as well as dozens of inexpensive package tours to exotic places such as Corfu and Tunisia and the Riviera in Spain.

If you are a student and you possess an international student travelling card, you are eligible to utilize the network of student flights throughout Europe. These are more inexpensive than any flights you will find through travel agents, and are just as reliable. You can obtain a listing of these flights from an international student center in the country you are in, or in the United States, consult your university travel center.

BUSES IN EUROPE. No generalizations can be made about European buses, as each country differs greatly. The "coach" tours in England are quite comfortable, and the people who take them are interesting and of all backgrounds. The English themselves take coach tours frequently.

However, taking buses in Spain, Portugal, Greece, or Italy would be quite uncomfortable and unreliable. The times of departure and arrival are never set, and many times, in those secluded little villages we cherish so, the buses simply leave when they have enough (sardine-like) passengers to pay for the trip and make a profit for the driver. If you depend on buses for these countries, though you will save money superficially, you may miss a scheduled plane or train, thus costing yourself extra money in the long-run.

TAKING YOUR CAR WITH YOU. Unless you are only interested in awing the natives, do not take your car with you. First of all, gasoline prices are often twice that of United States' pumps. Second, European roads are designed for smaller cars.

Third, if you have any trouble with your car overseas, odds are it will be very difficult (often out and out impossible) to fix, and very expensive at that.

Instead, rent or buy a car overseas. You'll save a lot of gasoline money (the average American sedan gets less than half the mileage a similar, albeit smaller, European model does) and avoid many other headaches.

CAR RENTALS. Sometimes, you can save a lot of money by renting a car when you are in another country, in addition to the advantages of coming and going when and where you please.

For example, take the Caribbean countries. In a country like St. Martin, it is well within the realm of reality for one to spend forty dollars a day on taxis. The car rental rates, with unlimited mileage, range from ten to twenty-five dollars a day, and offer the convenience of having a vehicle at your instant disposal.

It's important to check and see if the country you plan to visit and drive in will honor your American driver's license. Furthermore, when riving in rural areas of any country, the situation in case of accident can be most uncomfortable if no local authority can read or speak English.

What to do? If you are driving to Latin America, obtain an Inter-American license from the government, or from the American Automobile Association (AAA) for usually about five dollars plus two photos. Service is available to non-members for the same fee. If your driving will be in Europe, obtain an International Driving Permit, which is really just a translation of pertinent information into several languages. They are required in Spain, Portugal, Austria, Germany and

Italy.

In Great Britain, car rentals can be a real bargain. Go to the British Yellow Pages and make a few phone calls to suburban and rural car renters. Never rent from a tourist area, such as downtown London, the West End, or Queensway. Find a rate you can afford, take a bus to that location and rent a car there. Car rentals in suburban London go for as little as seventy dollars a week plus a small deposit. In the northern areas, of course, the rental fees will be much less.

Please remember that automatic transmissions are hard to come by in Europe, so if you plan to rent a car, be sure it's one you can handle.

Always rent your car in Europe and not in the United States through a travel agent; it must seem easier certainly to know that you will have a car waiting for you in France arranged by your travel agent, rather than having to deal with speaking to the French rental office yourself, but you will save yourself a minimum of fifty dollars if you do it yourself in Europe.

NOTE: some countries on the continent are better for renting cars than others. The most expensive countries to rent cars are France and Switzerland. Spain is also high-priced because so few people have this luxury there. The West German car rentals are expensive, too, because their economy is in better shape compared to ours. However, the cheapest country to rent in is also the first one you will probably land in: the Netherlands. Helpfully, nearly every Dutch person speaks some English, and particularly so the person who work in car rental offices. Consequently your "ordeal" on negotiating your car will not be difficult at all. They are friendly and helpful and their price is the cheapest. Also inexpensive is car rental in Luxembourg.

Another possible money-saver is the fly-drive package. Most fly-drive packages feature accommodations for one night in the gateway (starting) city. We advise that you take the free room on your last night in that country (city)...you'll be relaxed for your flight home, and you'll be right near the airport.

Plan your ride trip with an accurate map before leaving the United States. Write to the tourist office of the country you plan to visit to obtain a good map. It is strongly recommended that you obtain a Michelin Guide or a Blue Guide because they steer you to the historic places, recommend the right restaurants, and even indicate whether or not the facility has a parking lot! Also, these guides are clear when it comes to the maps. You will never get lost following the map of a Michelin. The Blue Guides are particularly good in describing a city center for the driver, and also the historical/educational features they offer are rich and varied.

Drive as you would when touring the United States. In other words, figure on 120 to 160 miles a day, at an average speed of thirty-five miles an hour, except on the super highways. On these, be prepared for the high speeds of up to ninety miles an hour!

Make sure you obtain a full collision damage insurance with the car—it costs a few extra dollars (sometimes a few cents, depending on the country) and is worth it because you will avoid the hassles of any bumps or scratches picked up along the way...and Europeans are known for their recklessness.

BUYING A CAR OVERSEAS. In contrast to rentals, outright purchases should be arranged before you go over there. There are two popular types of purchases, outright and planned-resale.

An outright purchase is exactly that. You will buy a car in Europe or wherever you happen to be going, and it is yours to do with as you please. If you plan to bring it back to the United States, make sure it is factory equipped with all of the new American safety standards or it will not be allowed through customs (unless you agree to make the modifications here—a very costly process). Also, be prepared to pay outrageous rates for freighter space, and be sure to purchase marine stevedore insurance as protection against the atrociously ungentle handling given to cars.

Furthermore, if you plan to bring your new car home with you, here are several other factors to consider:

1. Great Britain requires export of cars to be made with twelve months of purchase.

2. Payments must be made in hard currency (dollars, pounds, marks, French or Swiss francs) on the spot—there are no plans or layaways.

3. Many foreign dealers sell "new" cars which are not brand new. Some governments allow the "new" label to be put on a car if it has less than five thousand miles on it! Be sure to check and make sure the car is a BRAND NEW car.

4. The United States duty on automobiles is three percent.

5. Private resale of cars is virtually non-existent in Europe because of the huge taxes laid on such sales. The lowest resale tax is in France, where it is a "mere" twenty percent!! And stay out of Andorra's tax free car sale trap. The buyers there know all about the taxes elsewhere, and are more than ready to pull the old rip-off on the unsuspecting.

6. Most foreign insurance companies will not

accept applicants under twenty-one years of age.

7. Brokerage rates are assessed on top of freighting charges when you go to send the auto home.

However, there is a reasonable alternative which will save you lots of money. THE PLANNED RESALE PACKAGE. This deal is self-explanatory. You buy a brand new car, and as part of the sale, the car dealer arranges for you to sell it back to him, tax free. The repurchase price is agreed upon in advance and put into writing so there is no hanky-panky at the end.

There are many companies offering this service, and surprisingly enough, almost all of them are legitimate. A good one is Menet Auto Service International, in Jamaica, New York. This company is a leader in the field. It painstakingly explains its rates and resale programs, and is virtually complaint-free. Its explanatory brochure touches on every possible area, from accidents to radios. If you are interested in the planned resale package, they're the people to contact first.

BICYCLING IN EUROPE. Are you in good physical condition? Do you enjoy riding a bicycle? If you answered yes, then you should consider the bicycle as a fine alternative to gasoline-fed transportation. France, in particular, pushes the bicycle as a tourist transit method. More than eighty French railroad stations have bicycles for rent at five to seven dollars a day plus a small deposit, usually less than fifty dollars. And, as a real saver, if you bring your own bike, French trains will transport it as baggage for less than five dollars. Contact the French Tourist Agency listed in the end of this book for a list of the eighty-plus stations which offer this service, and for further details about bike tours across France.

HITCHHIKING ACROSS EUROPE. If you are willing to thumb for rides in the United States, there's no reason to drop the habit overseas, give or take a country. Many countries, particularly in Europe, the Middle East, South Africa and Australia-New Zealand are veritable hitchhiker's paradises. The value of this well-used form of transportation is obvious—its cost is minimal and you will meet the locals.

Where to hitchhike: England and the British Isles are safe, France is safe. Spain is questionable, but Portugal is quite safe. The Scandinavian countries are fine and the drivers are usually interesting, but you can get caught in some unexpected and torrential rainstorms, even in the summer, that might ruin your trip. I would avoid the Germanic countries, such as Austria and Germany, as the drivers there tend not to stop as readily as they do in Luxembourg, Belgium, and Holland.

Here are some hitchhiking hints:

1. If you are female, never hitchhike. It's just too dangerous, especially if you are not familiar with the male-female customs of the country you are in. For example, in certain countries, if a man makes advances to a woman and she vigorously rejects them, it is actually a symbol that she is interested! There are too many stories of rapes and robberies of women in overseas newspapers. Saving money is our objective, so a word to the wise should save money...and lives!

2. Spread a small replica of the American flag over your luggage, or, even better, your state flag. This is a guaranteed attention-getter, and the state flag will undoubtedly be unknown to the drivers picking you up, making you something of a

curiosity piece.

3. Carry only one piece of luggage. You will not be picked up if you have a wardrobe with you.

4. Carry at least one or two packs of American cigarettes with you. They make excellent, inexpensive gifts to benevolent drivers, and will put you in good standing.

5. Never hitchhike at night. Most European roads are not as well lit as their American counterparts.

6. Hold up a large, hand-drawn, easily seen and read sign indicating your destination.

7. Dress neatly. If you were driving would you pick up someone wearing rags?

8. Analyze the person who offers you a ride immediately. You must be careful about whom you trust, because they will be in control of your person and life for a while.

9. Be sure to obey the rules of hitchhiking. First, check to see if it's legal. At the time of this writing, it had been outlawed in a few European states.

Also, learn the hitchhiker's rules for the country you are seeking the ride in. Some European hitching stops have actual lines...and some of those lines work backwards!

10. The best hitchhiker's havens are of course, the roads, but don't be afraid to take a shot at boats, barges, and even airplanes at small airports. Very often, the drivers enjoy the company a foreigner brings. For some, it is the only contact with Americans they ever have.

The best way to use this method of transportation is on again off again. Don't try to do the whole trip on a hitchhiking basis; it is too exhausting, and you won't be able to enjoy any of those exotic places you are speeding through. Rather, after you arrive on the continent, use it to go from city to city, and even country to country. This way, you can travel light for a few days at a time, and save on transportation costs, while leaving most of your gear at your hotel room as your "base."

THE TAXI. "All generalizations are lies, including this one" is another way of saying that you should not characterize an entire group as good or bad. One "shyster" lawyer doesn't make all lawyers crooks. But, we feel obligated to go out on a limb and say that we've met too many crooked cab drivers from coast to coast, country to country, and continent to continent.

With real apologies to all of the hard-working underpaid honest cab drivers of the world, I will now relate the bad.

Remember, you are a foreigner in the country you are visiting. You are at the mercy of almost anyone who wants to take you for a ride if you do not speak the native tongue. Your request to go to the shopping area may be intentionally misunderstood; or as is more likely the case, the route chosen by the driver will be unnecessarily long.

So how do you fight back? First, use only authorized, government-licensed cabs. This means, take the time to look for an official sticker or window-certificate denoting a public hack. Make sure that the cab has a meter, with clearly printed rates.

Second, if you do not speak the local language, it is proper to hand the cab driver a slip of paper with the address you are going to, and ask him the price. It is also an excellent idea to ask one or two people at your hotel what it should cost to make the trip by public transportation, as well as by taxi.

Third, if there is any kind of an argument about the fare demanded upon arrival, ask to call a policeman, or if one is nearby, call him over yourself. Most licensed cabbies want nothing to do with the police; they much prefer to stay out of trouble with the local law. After all, they do have a license which has to be renewed (in some countries, licenses expire once every three months); and it is their only way of making a living, in most cases.

Fourth, carry small bills and coins, and make sure they are in the local currency. There are countless stories of drivers who have little or no change, especially when you are paying in dollars. (Despite the recent fluctuations on the world markets, every foreign business wants all of the dollars it can get its hands on!)

Fifth, keep in mind that taxis do not cruise the streets in many countries, especially at night. Be sure to check on the street availability of cabs after dark. If they are not cruising, be sure to arrange for one to pick you up at a specific time. And, if your destination is an out of the way place, make sure you've got transportation firmed up coming and going.

Many countries forbid cruises by cabs. Instead, you have to go to a taxi stand, much as you would a subway station or a bus stop. Amsterdam is an example. Learn the locations of these stands before you leave or go walking long distances.

Sixth, if you have any doubts about the city cab service, have the doorman at the hotel get a cab for you. It is worth the twenty-five cent tip to know you are getting an honest ride. And, when it's time to return to the hotel, do not be afraid to call the hotel and ask them to send a cab to your location.

Now that you know how to protect yourself from cabbies, it's time to consider their value as a means of getting around. As we have already stated, you can use up a great deal of your budget by the methods you choose to get around the country you are visiting. Some countries have notoriously high taxi rates, especially when compared to the cost of renting a car. In other countries, the reverse is true.

You can begin to decide your method of transportation as soon as your plane lands and you check the cab rates from the airport to your destination. For example, a taxi from the airport to your hotel may be less expensive than the bus service, especially if there are more than two people in your group. Avoid private cars and cabs offering to give you a tour en route to your hotel—they offer problems of both safety and cost.

When you decide how to travel once you arrive at your destination, make sure that whatever route you plan you don't retrace your steps. Let's say you are Berlin-bound by way of Paris. Your return plans call for a stop in Paris, too. But why stop twice in the same place, when you can stop in Amsterdam, Brussels, or London for no more than forty dollars extra? Furthermore, if you do set up a "circle trip," most transportation companies will offer a ten percent discount.

Circle trips can be used everywhere. You might fly from Boston to Los Angeles, up to Vancouver and then back to Boston. You could sail from Miami to the Grand Bahamas, fly to Luxembourg, take a train to Brussels, and fly back to the United States.

They also offer another advantage: you need not actually make the extra stop if you do not want to, and you still get the discount. Just make the stop in the extra airport and then board the next plane to your next destination.

TRAVEL FOR FREE. Everyone's dream is to win a free vacation for two to wherever their heart desires.

And that dream can be transposed into reality in several different ways. Or, at least, you can get there for free, especially if your destination is in the continental United States.

Many people see the U.S.A. the freebie way each year. Best of all, they see the country while riding in plush, top-quality cars. Their technique: dead-heading, or the so-called auto forwarding services. Just look in the yellow pages under Auto Forwarding.

The usual arrangement is that you will deliver (drive) a car to a particular city where the owner wants it. You are given free use of the car in exchange for delivering it, and in many cases, you can talk the service into paying for your gas and tolls! As a matter of fact, we've successfully negotiated gas, tolls, and some expenses along the way, as company costs!

Let's take an example. Mr. Jones in Las Vegas plans to go to Miami for a few months, and does not want to be without the use of his own car. He goes to the Auto Forwarding Service in Las Vegas and pays to have his car driven to Miami while he flies there. The service is usually expensive, so most owners are there to transport Cadillacs, Lincolns, Mercedes, etc. Imagine driving cross-country in a BMW 530!

Often, the service can arrange for you to have a car to drive back to your home town if you want to make it a round trip. Needless to say, the cost of getting there is minimal, leaving some the cash to really enjoy themselves and others an opportunity to go on a vacation they would otherwise never take.

Here are a couple of extra hints:

1. Always make sure that the car has been checked out by the service before you drive it, they should

give you a certificate saying the car is "healthy," and authorizing you to charge repairs on a special account.

2. Invest in the major classified ad newspaper in the nearest very large city. That's where these services usually advertise.

3. Make sure you have plenty of time so you can drive at a leisurely pace and stop off at will, and thus avoid eating at the on-the-highway restaurants (the biggest rip-offs in the business) because you are pressed for time.

Would you believe you can fly to Monaco, the Caribbean Islands, Nevada for FREE if you are really a gambler?

Gambling can be the best passport money can earn. Free junkets to the luxurious new Loews Monte Carlo (Monaco) gives seven days, six nights for two; room, all food, beverages, valet, tips, tax, transfers, etc.—and it's all win or lose.

To be invited, you must complete a special credit application. Approval will be based upon the size of your personal and business checking accounts (five thousand dollar minimum).

Or you can make a "front money" deposit of $7,500, borrow against it to gamble, and then take the remainder or appreciation home at no charge.

At Monte Carlo you are expected to bet at least twenty-five to fifty dollars a shot. A satisfactory player is one who spends about three solid hours a night betting...so if you are not this kind of player, do not go. If you don't bet up to expectations, the "house" has the option of charging you for expenses, and you will not be invited back. The house will get "ripped-off" only once.

In Puerto Rico and Aruba, you are expected to draw at least five hundred dollars minimum each night.

Bahama Casino Tours (888 Seventh Avenue, New York City) offers a unique twelve-hour casino tour. You leave at 6 p.m., return at 6 a.m.; tour features two two-hour plane rides, dinner, breakfast, drinks, show, and gratuities. You pay under one hundred dollars for a seat reservation and must bring seven hundred dollars "front money". Front money for Las Vegas should be substantially more.

The following are some gambling freebie operators:

Viking Tours
130 West 42nd Street
New York, New York 10036

Island Casino Tours
35 East Wacker Drive
Chicago, Illinois 60601

Global Sporting Club
7009 Coldwater Canyon
North Hollywood, California 90028

It's always great to take a tax-deductible vacation, and there are two ways to do it. The first is common: take a vacation related to your employment and claim the trip was for educational purposes, or designed to enhance your knowledge of the field in which you are employed. An example of this might be that a professor of French history can take a trip to France to "study" the cultural history of Marsellaise—with stops in Paris and Versailles, of course!

The second choice is to join a scientific or

sociological expedition. Several universities send them out, staffed with experts, and a handful of volunteers who make a prescribed donation (tax deductible, of course) and are willing to really rough it with hard work. No previous experience is necessary, there is no upward age limit, and the only qualification is a desire to learn about another culture.

To get in on this opportunity, contact the larger universities and colleges in your state, and in other states. The University of California at Berkeley runs several of these expeditions every year. Contact the University Research Expeditions Program, in care of the University Herbarium, Department of Botany, University of California, Berkeley, California 94720. Donations range from five hundred to fifteen hundred dollars, but are tax deductible.

The other alternative is to pay your way there, and stay someplace for free. The Servas Organization offers this unique opportunity, but first you must join the organization and be interviewed for travel. The fees for this amount to under fifty dollars. If you pass, and most people do, you will have the opportunity to go abroad, and upon arrival, stay in the home of a foreign family, gratis, provided you are willing to experience them on a one-to-one basis for a few days.

The organization is non-political, and has a list of 32,000 hosts worldwide expecting visitors who will "bring the rest of the world to them" because they cannot afford to go on foreign vacations.

The concept may sound crazy, but the organization is reliable, although under-fianced. Their address is Servas U.S., 11 John Street, New York, New York.

FREEBIES FOR THE RETIRED MILITARY. One benefit of making the armed forces a career is the Military Airlift Command, a non-IATA airline which offers free transportation across the United States or overseas for retired military men and women.

To obtain space on a flight to your vacation destination, contact Space Available Information Center, 1811 State Street, Box 359, Santa Barbara, California.

SAVINGS FOR SENIOR CITIZENS. You should be travelling during the Golden Years, not sitting around on some beach or wasting your time at an adult home. Age is no reason to stop travelling, unless your health prevents it.

Many other Americans who desire to travel will be surprised at the variety of savings most other countries offer to seniors. In some cases, these benefits were designed for that country's elderly, but in all cases, they are open to you.

To claim these senior discounts, you must bring proof of your age with you. Since any American abroad has his or her passport, you are already carrying this proof with you. If you are in Canada, a driver's license or Medicare Card is always acceptable.

Here is a list of money-savers open to travellers who are members of the senior set as defined by each country:

Austria. Women over sixty and men over sixty-five are eligible to choose between two plans, with preference based on your length of stay in Austria. You can buy an identification card at any Austrian railroad station, which brings a fifty percent discount on the national railway and on most private railways, and on buses. These cards are not honored during July and August, nor on weekends or holidays, except on local lines. (The Austrian weekend rate begins on Friday.)

Great Britain. All Britons receive reduced rate on transportation and many admissions after their sixtieth birthday. There is no standing policy extending this courtesy to foreigners, but in most cases, if you show proof of age, you'll be treated the same as any Briton.

Britain's private businesses offer many discounts for seniors. SAGA Senior Citizens Holidays, Ltd., 119 Sandgate Road, Folkstone, Kent, England, offers anyone over sixty membership in its senior organization for about one dollar annually. Members get to participate in a wide variety of one-week and two-week vacations, which are run in conjunction with British Rail and are very inexpensive. Another advantage is that these vacations are designed for English seniors—so you will get a real taste of English life, and meet some very interesting people.

Another advantage of travelling in England is the free medical treatment which is offered there to anyone who cannot afford to pay. For a list of many other discounts and specials for seniors, contact the British Tourist Authority at 680 Fifth Avenue, New York, New York.

Canada. Here, the age of advantage is sixty-five, and includes a ten to twenty percent travel discount on the Canadian National Railway on fares of more than six dollars. The bus service in Newfoundland offers the same discounts, but Canadian Pacific Railway does not. In the provinces of Quebec and Ontario, the Voyager Bus Line offers a fifty percent discount to seniors when the tickets are worth two dollars or more.

Denmark. Tourists over sixty-five can buy railroad tickets and bus round-trip tickets for fifty percent off on any trip covering twenty miles or more, except on weekends and during Easter and Christmas.

Finland. If you are more than sixty-five years old, you can buy a senior railway ticket for about one dollar fifty, which offers you an opportunity to then purchase up top six rail tickets—at half price—for trips of more than thirty-one miles. A "pensioner's" discount on domestic flights cuts twenty-five percent off Finnair's rates.

Luxembourg. Those over sixty-five receive a fifty percent discount on all buses and trains.

France. One thing the French do is cater to the seniors, defined as women of sixty and men of sixty-five. For a small fee, you can buy a Carte Vermel at any railroad station and you will save up to thirty percent on trail fares for one year. Unfortunately, there are numerous restrictions which change from month to month, so check them out when you buy your card. People in the same age group will also get a twenty-five percent discount on Air Inter, the French domestic airline, but once again, there are restrictions. Museums and other landmarks offer half-price admissions to seniors.

Norway. A senior citizen is defined as a person who is at least sixty-seven years of age, and is allowed a fifty percent discount on train tickets for trips of more than thirty-one miles. Some private steamers also offer discounts.

Switzerland. The absolute best country for seniors. For under fifty dollars, men over sixty-five and women over sixty-two can buy a one-half Fare Travel Card in the United States or in Switzerland good on any regularly scheduled train, including the

74

world-famous mountain railroads, Swiss buses and lake steamers. More than that, it leads to reduced rates at most hotels—just present it on arrival.

There are all sorts of other discounts...most restaurants offer twenty 'percent off to seniors...most theatres offer similar discounts, etc.

Spain. For just a few cents, a sixty-five year old can buy a one-year half-fare ticket good on any government railway in Spain during off seasons.

Sweden. Your sixty-fifth birthday is cause to celebrate in Sweden because it brings a fifty percent discount on train tickets, some buses, and some ferries operated by the State (except weekends in June, July and August, and during Easter and Christmas).

The Netherlands. Another senior special country, offering a half-fare transit card for just a few dollars good on trains and buses. More importantly, the card is a discount-bringer (usually fifty percent) at many museums and public institutions.

West Germany. Men and women of sixty-five and sixty, respectively, get a forty percent discount on round-trip train tickets on condition that the distance is more than thirty-two miles. A fifty percent discount is given on buses.

Round trip flights between Berlin and many other parts of the country are available at special savings for seniors.

Reduced admissions for seniors are usually in effect at palaces and castles, especially in Bavaria. Always show your proof of age and ask...it cannot hurt.

Finally, join the American Association of Retired Persons. For just a few dollars a year, you'll open the door to inexpensive, extensive vacations to Spain, Morocco, Mexico, and Italy. Very often, savings are fifty percent or more for deluxe vacations. Their address is: American Association of Retired Persons, 1909 K Street, N.W., Washington, D.C. 20049.

Unfortunately, some countries make no provisions for seniors...and others refused to respond to our inquiries. Once you are there, always ask about senior discounts because it often works.

IV

WHAT TO TAKE

You are ready to go: you know how you are going, where you are going, and how you will get around once you are there, all in the cheapest way possible. Packing for a trip is essential, difficult, and frustrating. You can't live day to day without certain items, yet which ones? Will it really be a hassle to take that extra suitcase? And once you fill up your luggage you realize that you will have nothing in which to carry home all those lovely presents and purchases for yourself that you are going to make abroad. You pack and unpack; you sit on the suitcase in order to force it closed and realize that one heavy throw from an airline employee will send your baggage reeling open across the airport floor.

What should you take? For a week, for a month, for the summer? By car or by plane?

There is one general rule to remember when packing. If in doubt, leave it out. Take as little as possible. Remember, you are on vacation, not moving to the place you are travelling. You don't need nine shirts, fourteen ties, six lightweight jackets, and two frying pans. Leave the crate of lemons home.

Hand in hand with the trend towards over-luggaging, most travellers pack a wardrobe fit only for a king. You just don't need it.

A reasonable wardrobe includes lightweight clothing for the hot summer days, cottons and "breathable" synthetics, a raincoat for the European summer rain. Certainly not your winter boots or your heavy wools. The following list comprises a reasonable wardrobe, and one that should fit into one large suitcase. Remember, even the luggage with wheels is hard to handle at airports and making boat changes. ANY LUGGAGE IS INCONVENIENT, when you are rushing from one mode of transportation to another, when you are walking the streets of a foreign city looking for a hotel room, and heavy luggage, or more than one piece, is unbearable. Never take more than you yourself can carry. COMFORTABLY. When you are trudging the endless corridors of the boat-train Paris to London changeover, and you are carrying your luggage and you are dead tired, you will wish you'd left behind that extra piece.

General

Shoulder bag	Shaver
Folding umbrella	Small clothesline
Bathrobe	Foot powder
Folding Slippers	Shower cap
Shoe-trees	Shampoo
Shoe-shine	Washcloth
Plastic bags	Toothbrush and paste
Kleenex	Travel iron
Sewing kit	Wash 'n' Dries
First aid kit	Eye lotion
Medicines	Eye mask
Nail clippers	Deodorant
Soap and case	Personal Toiletries
Nail file	Radio
Insect repellant	Sunglasses
Ear stoppers	Extra eyeglasses

Men

Raincoat with lining
Two suits
Sports jacket
Sweater
Two pairs of slacks
Four dress shirts
Sports shirt

Three ties
Bermuda shorts
Undershorts
Beach jackets
Two bathing suits
Undershirts
Pajamas

Women

Raincoat with lining
One suit
Sweater set
Pair of slacks
Two skirts
Two blouses
Sheath/jacket
Head scarf

Bermuda shorts
Panties
Beach jacket
Two bathing suits
Bras
Nightgown
Two daytime dresses
Two evening dresses

Both men and women
Thongs/sandals
Dress shoes (one pair)
Belt
Walking shoes
Tennis or jogging shoes
Five pairs of socks/stockings

And that should do it. Of course, if you're going to Norway for a ski vacation, you can leave the shorts at home and take the appropriate winter garb in place of the summer stuff.

V.

CHECKLIST

Now that you have packed conservatively, and you know that carrying your luggage will not be a problem, there are certain final arrangements you must make before you leave. The following is a personal checklist to put your regular, day-to-day life on a stop-hold while you are gone:

CHECKLIST FOR DEPARTURE

1. Stop routine services: including newspapers, milk and any other food deliveries, laundry, and refuse collection.

2. Arrange acceptance for non-cancellable deliveries and have a neighbor take in your mail. Do not have the post office hold your mail—one of the easiest ways for burglars to "case" a house and learn its occupants are away is to watch where the mailman does not stop. Also, you might want to arrange with a friend to come and stay at your house once a week, on a different day each week, or to come in each morning and each evening and turn different lights on or off for the day or night, in order to "fool" the burglars.

3. Cancel personal and business appointments. It's a good idea if you have regular clients at work to

notify them casually, in your correspondence with them, that you are planning a vacation from a certain date and will be out of the office until the return date. In this way, they won't waste their time, and they won't become frustrated that they can't get hold of you.

4. Local police should be notified of your absence.

5. Arrange any pet care needed. And remember, this does not merely mean that someone come in and feed your pets. If you are going away for more than two weeks, you will need to make arrangements for your pets to have proper exercise and proper company. Many animals who are used to human companionship become listless and develop illnesses when they are suddenly plunged into a solitary environment.

6. Arrange for lawn and garden care, or snow removal.

7. Arrange to have house plants watered.

8. Check expiration dates on insurance policies.

9. Store furs, valuables, and documents in a safe place.

10. Shut off gas and electricity if practical.

11. Set thermostat on low; do same for boiler. Shut off air conditioners.

12. Lock windows, doors, basement, garage, and connect security lights inside and out. It is wise to purchase one or two lamp-timers—which will automatically turn lights on and off in your house.

13. Empty your refrigerator and defrost it; then, set it on off and leave the door open. Arrange for a neighbor or friend to turn it back on the day before you return.

14. Remove flammable materials from your home.

15. Leave house, car, and office keys with a friend

or relative, along with a copy of your itinerary. Ask your friend to be sure to start your car up every two or three days, and to change its position on the driveway or in the lot.

16. Advise someone of your vault and safe arrangements, any lawyers and doctors of importance, and where your emergency keys are kept.

17. Check your luggage well in advance, and mark it clearly with your name, home address, and destination. This gives added protection against loss in transit, and enables the carrier to forward your luggage to the proper destination.

Once you have taken care of those items, pay attention to the items below which deal with matters connected with your trip:

CHECKLIST FOR OVERSEAS

1. Get your passport and passport case early. It takes about two weeks from the time of application until the time you receive your passport in the mail. But remember, just before the peak travelling seasons, the period of waiting will stretch out to accommodate all the people who are applying for passports, so be sure to allow yourself plenty of time. If you do not have your passport you simply cannot leave the country (except to go to Mexico or Canada), and this is a sure way to ruin your vacation if you have not yet received your passport by your date of departure.

2. Acquire those visas which are less expensive when purchased outside your destination. And be sure to check with the embassy of each country you intend to visit, to see if you will need a visa for that country, and find out how long it takes to acquire them. For most European countries on this side of

the Iron Curtain, the visa is stamped directly in your passport the day you cross the frontier; there is no application made and no waiting. However, certain Communist countries require application and charge fees.

3. Obtain any required information, and a World Health Certificate.

4. Write down your itinerary and keep the list somewhere convenient. A good idea is to keep it with your traveller's checks.

5. Bring you driver's license; acquire any necessary driving information or special licenses or insurance the country may require.

6. Put your tickets, transfers, travellers checks and credit cards in a handy place.

7. Obtain foreign money at a bank or the airport before you leave. Certainly you will be able to change money at your destination, but the offices are not always open when you land, the lines are long if they are open, and you are always tired and in a hurry to get to your hotel and rest from the long journey. So it is a good idea to have some money changed before you leave to get you into a taxi, airport limousine, etc., and to the airport, until you can get to a bank. Also, if you are landing on a weekend, remember to have more changed to get you through the weekend.

8. Purchase travel insurance from your travel agent or at the airport. This can be done at a counter at the airport before your flight takes off, or in the larger cities, machines have now taken the place of the insurance salesperson.

9. Arrange transportation to and from the airport. This is essential. There is nothing worse than landing in a foreign country, not having any sense of how far you are from the city or how to get

there. Know before you go how much an airport transfer vehicle will cost, have that money ready in their currency, and know how long it will take and who will handle your luggage while you are being transferred to your hotel.

10. Take an address book. Even the most experienced of travellers sends post cards; don't forget the list of addresses you will need for this.

VI

WEATHER:
What to Expect

How many times have you, or a friend, made that dream trip to wherever, to the Alps in summer (it rains), to Australia in December (it's HOT—their summer), to the Caribbean in July (the heat and humidity are unbearable then), only to find that the weather is not what you expected and intolerable, and ruins your trip? What a waste of time and money. And that's why I've included this convenient weather guide to Europe, North Africa, and the Middle East. Because I've been to Tyrol in the pouring rain when I expected gentle summer breezes...and I've been to Sydney expecting a mild Christmas and finding heat so unbearable that I cried for home...and because I've been to St. Croix for a summer holiday, only to find that the humidity was so high even the "natives" went elsewhere.

Spring/Fall:

Northern Europe	brisk days (40-60)	cool evenings (30-50)

Mid-Europe	cool days (50-60)	cool evenings (30-40)
Southern Europe	pleasant (60-75)	mild evenings (50-60)
North Africa	warm days (65-75)	cool evenings (40-60)
Middle East	warm-cool (60-75)	cool (40-65)

Summer:

Northern Europe	warm days (60-70)	cool evenings (50-60)
Mid-Europe	warm / hot (70-80)	pleasant (50-60)
Southern Europe	hot days (80-90)	warm evenings (65-75)
North Africa	hot days (80-90)	warm evenings (60-80)
Middle East	warm / hot (80-100)	pleasant / cool (60-75)

Winter:

Northern Europe	brisk day (30-45)	cold evenings (20-30)
Mid-Europe	brisk day (30-45)	cold evenings (20-45)
Souther Europe	mild day (45-60)	cool evenings (30-50)
North Africa	mild day (50-72)	cool evenings (35-50)
Middle East	cool day (50-60)	brisk evenings (35-48)

The rainy seasons in these areas differ widely from our own. While you would not expect a rainy day in the summer in California or in the mid-west, in Central Europe rain is quite frequent in the summer. The heavy seasons of rain in Europe are fall and winter; in North Africa and the Middle East they are fall, winter, and particularly early spring.

VII.

MAKING YOURSELF AT HOME

Once you find yourself in the country or continent of your dreams, you will find that everything is done differently there than at home. So how do you maintain your sanity and still enjoy yourself? Obviously, some amenities from home you will have to sacrifice when you are travelling, particularly if you are on the move quite a bit or if you are in a country with a living standard lower than the United States. However, most habits/possessions you are accustomed to can be transferred to foreign countries in order for you to feel comfortable, as comfortable as you would be in your own living room.

THE TELEPHONE. Certainly you will want to call home at least once, but before you do you should be aware that the high price of overseas phone calls will be even higher if you do it from your hotel. It is not only a dirty trick, it's downright chicanery, but almost every hotel puts a surcharge on any phone call you make from your room to the outside world. Often, these surcharges are unwritten or are based on the time units which are never revealed to the customer in a clear, concise writing, least of all, on your final bill.

At the time of this writing only three countries are actively policing their hotels' surcharge rates: Israel, Ireland, and Portugal. In Israel, you pay a flat rate on credit card and collect calls; twenty-five percent on switchboard calls, with a maximum surcharge of about ten dollars. The Portuguese agreement places a twenty-percent surcharge on all calls, to a maximum of a couple of dollars. In Ireland, the hotels are limited to a flat fee with credit cards and collect calls; and twenty-five percent on calls made through the switchboard, with a maximum.

The Scandinavian countries do a little better than the rest of Europe in policing this system of surcharges, but other countries simply don't have any control over what a hotel may charge you for calling overseas with one of their phones. For an eight dollar call, you may find yourself spending forty dollars from a hotel in England or France.

Make all calls from local phones, pay phones outside the hotel, or from the post office. If made from the hotel, make the call collect or use a credit card number to save money. If you wait to see the charges on your bill, you will almost certainly be charged at least twice what the call would have cost from a public phone box.

In the United States, Holiday Inn, Ramada Inn, Howard Johnson, etc., each charge certain subcharge rates based on their own form of unit time. Check it out before you call, or use your telephone credit card, or call collect if you use the hotel phone. Otherwise, walk down the block or over to a pay phone and save.

MAIL FROM HOME. For some people, stopping all mail delivery is just plain impossible.

They need the steady flow of mail, whether for business or other reasons. For others, there is always the need to be reached in case of any emergency. And, of course, if you plan on an extended stay, you certainly don't want those bills and dated letters piling up, unopened and unanswered.

In the past, most Americans have had their mail forwarded to the American Express Office nearest to their vacation spot. Of late, this practice has become less popular, and with good reason. One problem is that this can be time-consuming and inconvenient. Another is that American Express is beginning to act more and more as a business corporation and less of an extension of the American Embassy. Many offices will only hold mail for clients, and the definition of client is sometimes not as obvious to clerks as it is in the minds of customers. Third, American Express will not hold messages for you; they will only hold regular, postmarked mail. In some cities, if you carry American Express Travelers Checks, this is good enough for the office to hold and hand over to you your mail. But in other cities, you must be an American Express Card carrying member in order to receive this service.

The growing alternative is to send messages and forward mail directly to the hotels you plan to stay at. Simply have the sender print "Hold for arrival on _____ (date)," and be sure to write out the month and date, because 6/1/81, in most European countries, means January 6, 1981!

If you do not have reservations, select a large hotel, and have the mail sent there. Most high quality hotels will hold the mail for you, even if you are not actually booked there. Then, periodically stop by to collect whatever has arrived.

Another possibility is to send the mail care of the American Embassy and to mark it similarly. The major drawback to this method is that it might get lost in government communications, or might be thrown out by accident if too much mail accumulates.

Of course, if you have a business brunch, bank office, or friend or relative at your destination, your problem is solved. You'd be surprised at the number of people who go overseas to visit someone and fail to use that person's address as a forwarding location.

ELECTRICAL GADGETS. The English have a standing joke about the dumb Yanks who come over to the motherland with their electric razors, televisions, and radios. It basically talks about how the American in question bragged for hours about his/her great appliance, plugged it into a wall socket for all to see, was bet by one or two natives that the gadget would not work, and then lost his shirt. Impossible, you say. No, not at all, because in many other countries the wall socket voltage is substantially higher than it is in America. You plug in your handy razor, turn it on, and boom!

A word to the wise: always check out the electrical rating of any socket you plan to use. If you don't, you may indeed get the shock of your life, and be left without a valuable personal appliance which you will then have to spend a lot of money to replace. If you do blow out an appliance, and you plan to travel through Germany, try to wait until you reach that country before replacing it, as most electrical appliances are cheaper in that country.

Do not use U.S. 110 volt rated appliances in Europe without a converter or unless you are sure that it is also 110 volt outlet. It is the case that many high quality hotels have both socket offerings for their guests, because they host so many American guests. However, most hotels in Europe do not offer this. Instead, before you leave, buy a converter. They are compact and easy to carry. They will cost you between twenty-five and thirty dollars, and they will last for life on every trip you take. I find them well worth the price. They are obtainable in any department store, from many hadrware stores, and also from Communications House; Dobbs Ferry, New York 10522.

HOTELS. Hotels throughout the world are very different from those we know here in the United States. When an American thinks of a hotel, he thinks generally of either a traditional Miami hotel for resort luxury, or a posh, classy New York hotel in the center of downtown Manhattan. If you share that picture, you will join the ranks of thousands of American tourists who are greatly disappointed when they go overseas.

Of course, American hoteliers are aware of the American picture of what a hotel should be, and their answer has been to build exact replicas of the American-style hotel in Europe and the Far East. In keeping with their American predecessors, they are very plastic and extremely expensive, and all you will get for your money is an American hotel with American designs for American tastes.

The real way to travel overseas is to do it the same way the natives do. In other words, you should stay in the same hotels and inns the locals would if they were travelling. For example, in Europe, look for accommodations posted with the words Pension or Zimmer. These are guides to hotel accommodations at reasonable prices, often as low as four to six dollars a night. Be forewarned that in Europe, first-class means the equivalent of American second-class. To get American first-class quality, you have to look for the word "deluxe". However, these cheaper hotels are clean, efficient, and smaller usually, so you will have the chance to talk with other guests during your stay, many times other guests from other parts of the country you are visiting. There is no reason to pay seventy-five dollars a night for a hotel room where you meet no one but the hall porter, when you could be paying five dollars for a homier place where you meet and become friends with a family of Europeans.

It is important when renting a hotel room in other parts of the world that you see the room before you sign for it, or pay for it. Many fine guest houses have desirable and undesirable rooms, frequently at the same price. By asking to see your room first, you will find out whether or not it meets your standards, and sometimes you will be given a better room because you asked to see the room in advance.

Another key consideration when picking a room is fire—its prevention and plan of action if one occurs. Are the doors made out of thin plywood, the furniture highly flammable? Are there no fire extinguishers in the hallways/no fire escapes outside the building? The object of this book is to save your travel dollars, and to have your belongings go up in smoke is the antithesis of our goal. In general, no matter where you are staying, ask about fire exits, and plot a method of escape in case of fire.

If you have a choice, take a room upstairs. The higher the better, and northeastern locations in the hotel are the most desirable. Height brings less noise, fewer insects, and cleaner air. The northeast is usually cooler. And remember, that overseas, the first floor is not on street level; it's one flight up. Their street level is either the ground floor or the lobby. Another reason to choose a room higher up, is that you will get a fine view of the city that way, and you will be able, from your hotel room window, to orient yourself to where you want to go sightseeing, without the encumbrance of bulky maps.

Keep in mind that only the deluxe hotels in Europe, and similarly the highest class on other continents, automatically offer such commonplace items as soap and air conditioning. Check to see if these, and other staples are included. In general, when travelling from hotel to hotel in Europe, you should take with you soap, toothpaste, and a towel, because you won't always find these things in the rooms.

And watch out for apparent freebies. If there is a bottle of champagne in your room, it may not be "on the house," especially in Austria, Spain, Portugal, and France. Make sure you ask if the item is free of charge—the owner will not be offended, because Europeans do the same thing, and will probably realize he is not dealing with typical dumb Americans, saving you from other attempts at milking money later on.

And remember, you can save on hotel bills if you are willing to sleep one night on a bus or train while travelling.

If you arrive in a foreign city with no reservations, look for a "hotel booking agency". These are particularly useful in Europe, and are usually found in bus stations, airports, and train stations. They are run by the host government, and so are perfectly respectable. For a small fee, of usually less than one dollar, they will telephone to find you a hotel. What's more, they keep trying until they find you a room in your price range. They are wonderful and friendly people to the tired, homeless tourist. They have special listings, constantly updated, of all the hotels in their city, and of which have rooms available, and because they are government run, all the hotels are checked for cleanliness and legitimacy. You may not be lodged in the best neighborhood in town, but you will be lodged at the price you ask for and with decent accommodations.

Another trick for savings at overseas hotels, particularly in Europe and the Middle East, is to join Budget Accommodations Systems, developed primarily for students, but open to anyone. Just show your BAS Directory at any listed hotel before 1 p.m., and you are guaranteed a room, plus a discount of from ten to fifty percent. The Directory costs under five dollars, and may be purchased by mail through either the Council on International Education, 777 United Nations Plaza, New York, New York 10017, or from 236 North Santa Cruz Street, Suite 314, Los Gatos, California.

When you travel in the United States, a handy number to keep with you is 800-AE8-5000. This is the American Express Space Bank phone number. The bank will, at no fee, provide confirmed reservations in hundreds of cities. Space bank rooms are sometimes a little more expensive, but it's a handy number for emergencies.

Another wise move when in the United States is to trek down to the local Holiday Inn, Ramada Inn, Hilton Hotel, or Howard Johnsons and take advantage of their free room reservation cables. They'll reserve you a room in the franchise hotel at your place of vacation at no charge (provided rooms are available, of course).

In the next few sections, alternative hotels will be discussed.

BUDGET MOTELS. You know the ad for budget hotels: "...and the price won't keep you awake." Many people are afraid of them because they suspect these establishments are little more than fleabags with rotten mattresses and no running water.

Yet, for the most part, they are clean and decent in the United States, and range from ten dollars for a single on up. You can expect a television, a telephone, modern furnishings, wall to wall carpeting, individual temperature control, swimming pool and ice. They usually accept credit cards and are conveniently located. They are also conspicuously absent from the big cities, but usually hide in nearby suburbs. So if you are driving the highways looking for a place to stay for the night, drive past the big cities for a stretch to see if you find any budget motel signs off the road a few miles beyond the center of the town. This can save you up to fifty dollars in the night's lodging price.

Here is a list of reliable, popular budget motel chains which we recommend. Write to them for their locations and franchises across the United States.

Motel 6. Although a mere fifteen years in existence, this is the oldest budget motel chain. More than thirty-six states are covered with two hundred and thirty-five properties containing Motel 6, except for the Northeast and California. Rates are under fifteen dollars a night for a single. Television is optional for a small fee, a few cents a day. No credit cards are honored. Write to Motel 6, 1888 Century Park East, Los Angeles, California 90067.

Swiss Chalet. This motel chain features twenty-one locations in the New England states. Toll-free reservations numbers...just call them in Nashua, New Hampshire, or write to Swiss Chalet, 2 Progress Avenue, Nashua, New Hampshire, 03060.

Red Roof Inns. Operate roughly thirty inns in seven midwestern states, principally in Michigan, Ohio and Indiana. Write to Red Roof Inns, Post Office Box 283, Columbus, Ohio 43216.

Penny Pincher and L-K Motels. Some fifty-seven locations in the Midwest, particularly in Ohio, Indiana, Michigan. There are toll-free reservation numbers. Write to 1125 Ellen Kay Drive, Marion, Ohio 43302.

Days Inns. The world's largest budget chain with two hundred and forty-two inns and thirty-three lodges, mostly in the South and Midwest. Plan to expand into Ontario, Canada more extensively. The lodges are slightly more expensive because they include kitchens. Toll-free numbers available. Write to Days Inns, 2751 Buford Highway, Northeast, Atlanta, Georgia 30324.

California 6 and Western 6. Twenty-nine locations in California and Arizona. Write to 1156 South Seventh Avenue, Hacienda Heights, California 91745.

COLLEGES AND UNIVERSITIES: CHEAP AND CLEAN. If someone told you that you could stay in a clean, spacious, air-conditioned room for less than two dollars a day during your visit to Belgium, you might wonder. If that same person told you that in certain Eastern European countries, you could have even better accommodations than that, for less than one dollar a day, you'd surely think the speaker was crazy.

Yet the incredible truth is that such

accommodations not only exist in more than forty-five countries around the world, but they usually come complete with low cost meals, free/low cost recreational opportunities, and daily social activities. Activities also include movies, theatres, ballets, observatories, canoeing, scuba diving...an almost endless variety of all the things people take vacations to experience.

Where does one discover these values? At the colleges and universities in every state in the United States, and similar institutions of higher learning around the world. Rooms usually range from two dollars to ten dollars, and meals start at an average of one dollar for breakfast, a full breakfast, and range up to two dollars fifty for dinner.

For the overseas traveller, simply contact the travel bureau or consulate of the countries which interest you if you are considering these kinds of accommodations. Or, when you arrive in the university towns (including, of course, all major European cities), look in the phone directory for the number of the university in that town and make a quick and simple call to find out how they rent out their rooms and if there are any available. This is common practice in foreign countries.

As for college and university lodging in the United States, consult partial lists presented below, or write to the college or university which you know to be conveniently located in relation to your travel plans. Contact the director of housing.

These listings are by state, and in no particular order.

ALABAMA
University of Alabama
contact: Cecil Givens, Assistant Director of

Housings, Department of Housing, 307 University Boulevard, Mobile, Alabama 36688 Phone: 205-460-6391

Tuskegee Institute
contact: T.W. Hardwich, in care of Residence Halls, Tuskegee Institute, Tuskegee, Alabama 36088

ALASKA
University of Alaska
contact: Russell S. Flaherty, Directory of Housing, Memorial Union, Alaska Student Union, Anchorage, Alaska

CALIFORNIA
Pitzer College
contact: Mrs. Vicke Selk; Scott Hall, 1150 Mills Avenue, Claremont, California 91711

University of California at Berkeley
contact: residence officer, International House, 2299 Piedmont Avenue, Berkeley, California 94720

Fresno State College
contact: Gail Griego, Conference Director, Fresno State College, Fresno, California

California State University
contact: Dr. John Heath, 6000 J Street, California State University of Sacramento, Sacramento, California 95825

San Francisco State University
contact: Verducci Hall, 770 Lake Merced Boulevard, San Francisco, California

COLORADO
Loretto Heights College
contact: Mr. Francis Kelley, Vice President for Administrative Operations, 3001 South Federal Boulevard, Denver, Colorado

CONNECTICUT
University of New Haven
contact: Mr. Phillip Robertson, Director of Housing and Student Center, 300 Orange Avenue, West Haven, Connecticut

FLORIDA
Marymount College
contact: Director of Conferences, Marymount College, Boca Raton, Florida

Florida Institute of Technology
contact: Florida Institute of Technology Vacation Center, Post Office Box 1150, Florida Institute of Technology, Melbourne, Florida

IDAHO
Idaho State College
1910 College Boulevard, Idaho State College, Boise, Idaho contact: Mr. J. Vestal, Director

ILLINOIS
Roosevelt University
contact: Mr. Larry Lund, Directory of Herman Crown Center, 425 South Wabash Avenue, Roosevelt University, Chicago, Illinois

Bradley University
contact: Jack Kuntz, Conference Director, Student Center, Bradley University, Peoria, Illinois

INDIANA
Indiana University
contact: Ross Smith, 801 North Jordan Avenue, Indiana University, Bloomington, Indiana

IOWA
University of Dubuque
contact: Larry Hook, Men's Housing Coordinator, University of Dubuque, Dubuque, Iowa

KANSAS
Kansas State College of Pittsburgh
contact: Housing Office, 112 Russ Hall, Kansas State College of Pittsburgh, Pittsburgh, Kansas

KENTUCKY
Spalding College
contact: Sr. Ann Leagey, Residence Director, Spalding College, Louisville, Kentucky

LOUISIANA
Loyola University
contact: Richard Lawton, Housing Director, 6363 St. Charles Avenue, Loyola University, New Orleans, Louisiana

MAINE
Bowdoin College
contact: Mrs. Mary C. Bernier, Hawthorne-Longfellow Hall, Bowdoin College, Brunswick, Maine

MARYLAND
Loyolla College
contact: Mrs. Margery W. Harriss, Coordinator of Special Events, 4501 North Charles Street, Loyolla College, Baltimore, Maryland

MASSACHUSETTS
Tufts University
contact: Mrs. Marjorie Farley McNiff, Director, Conference Bureau, Tufts University, Medford, Massachusetts

Curry College
contact: Robert Capalbo; 848 Brush Hill Road, Curry College, Milton, Massachusetts

MICHIGAN
Mercy College of Detroit
contact: Martha Weise, Director of Housing, 8200 West Outer Drive, Box 143, Mercy College, Detroit, Michigan

Northern Michigan University
contact: Housing Office, University Center, Northern Michigan University, Marquette, Michigan

MINNESOTA
College of St. Scholastica
contact: Director of Housing, Somers Hall, 1200 Kenwood Avenue, Duluth, Minnesota

MISSOURI
University of Missouri
contact: Mr. Van Miller, 5030 Cherry Street, University of Missouri, Kansas City, Missouri

Washington University
contact: Tootie Lewis, Coordinator, Conference and Guest Housing, 6516 Wydown Boulevard, St. Louis, Missouri

MONTANA
University of Montana
contact: Ronald Brunell, Assistant Director, Residence Halls, Missoula, Montana

NEBRASKA
Kearny State College
contact: Dan Duggy, Director of Housing, Kearny State College, Kearny, Nebraska

NEVADA
University of Nevada at Las Vegas
contact: Housing Office, 1130 University Boulevard, University of Nevada, Las Vegas, Nevada

University of Nevada, Reno
contact: Housing Office, 8034 Box Union Station, University of Nevada, Reno, Nevada

NEW HAMPSHIRE
University of New Hampshire
contact: Gail Tufts, Residence Office, Stoke Hall, University of New Hampshire, Durham, New Hampshire

NEW JERSEY
Montclair State College
contact: Lois Redd, Housing Services, Bohn Hall, Normal Avenue, Montclair State College, Montclair, New Jersey

NEW MEXICO
New Mexico Institute of Technology
contact: Kurt G. Krammer, Office of Student Affairs, Campus Station, Socorro, New Mexico

NEW YORK
Concordia College
contact: Housing Office, Concordia College, Bronxville, New York

Canisius College
contact: John Crabbe, Director of Residence Life, Bosch Hall, 2001 Main Street, Buffalo, New York

NORTH CAROLINA
Warren Wilson College
contact: Walter H. Kreamer, Business Manager, Warren Wilson College, Swannanoa, North Carolina

NORTH DAKOTA
Jamestown College
contact: Lloyd Peterson, Director of Business Affairs, Jamestown College, North Dakota

OHIO
University of Cincinnati
contact: Marion Haisley, Directory of Campus Calendar Office, 320 Tangeman, University Center, Cincinnati, Ohio

University of Dayton
contact: Edwin Melhuish, Director of Housing, 300 College Park, Dayton, Ohio

University of Toledo
contact: Housing Office, University of Toledo, Toledo, Ohio

OKLAHOMA
Southeastern State College
contact: William Morton, Southeastern State College, Durant, Oklahoma

OREGON
University of Portland
contact: Jan Tirrill, Villa Continuing Education Center, 5000 North Willamette Boulevard, Portland, Oregon

PENNSYLVANIA
Drexel University
contact: Housing Office, 203 North 34th Street, Drexel University, Philadelphia, Pennsylvania

Point Park College
contact: Francis J. Gruden, III, Director of Residence Halls, 201 Wood Street, Point Park College, Pittsburgh, Pennsylvania

RHODE ISLAND
University of Rhode Island
contact: Summer Housing Office, Manager of Dormitory Services, University of Rhode Island, Kingston, Rhode Island

SOUTH DAKOTA
University of South Dakota
contact: David Lorenz, Student Union, University of South Dakota, Springfield, South Dakota

TENNESSEE
Knoxville College
contact: Housing Office, 901 College Street, Knoxville, Tennessee

Tennessee State University
contact: Housing Office, 3500 Centennial Boulevard, Tennessee State University, Nashville, Tennessee

TEXAS
Bauder Fashion College
contact: Susan Huston, Public Relations, 508 South Center Street, Bauder Fashion College, Arlington, Texas

University of Dallas
contact: Brian Keller, Director of Housing, Box 73, University of Dallas, Irving, Texas

UTAH
University of Utah
contact: Mrs. Newman, Post Office Box 200, University of Utah, Salt Lake City, Utah

VERMONT
St. Joseph College
contact: St. Joseph College, Monument Road, Bennington, Vermont

Trinity College
contact: Sister Ruth Ravey, Colchester Avenue, Trinity College, Burlington, Vermont

VIRGINIA
Marymount College
contact: Marymount College, Housing Office, 2607 North Olebe Road, Arlington, Virginia

WASHINGTON
Eastern Washington State College
contact: Isabelle Green, Coordinator of Workshops and Conferences, Showalter, 308A, ODU, Eastern Washington State College, Washington

Seattle University
contact: Bernie Carvalho, Campion Tower, 914
East Jefferson, Seattle, Washington

WEST VIRGINIA
Marshall University
contact: Director of Housing, Old Main 126,
Marshall University, Huntington, West Virginia

WISCONSIN
University of Wisconsin
contact: Robert T. Seay, Conference Coordinator,
3400 North Maryland Avenue, University of
Wisconsin, Milwaukee, Wisconsin

It is important to remember that room
availability is usually decreased while the
college/university is in full session, but this will not
affect most travellers who travel during the late
spring, summer and fall.

Other factors to consider:

1. Some colleges only allow students as
temporary visitors, so indicate an educational
affiliation (e.g. taking night courses at the local
community college).

2. Most allow no pets and no alcoholic beverages.

3. When contacting any of the above colleges, or
any which are not listed, ask for a descriptive
brochure giving all the necessary information. Do
not be afraid to ask about any restrictions they
might have.

4. Always ask if the rate includes meals. This is the
case about half of the time.

5. Find out if the doors are locked at a certain
curfew hour. Occasionally, this is the case, the most
common curfew being eleven o'clock. Sometimes it

is later, at midnight, but in a few colleges it is at ten o'clock, and you need to know this before you decide to go out to a late movie, or you may find yourself locked out of your room.

6. Check out college-sponsored events during your stay, and also see if the college provides free or inexpensive transportation into, and around, the city or town.

7. Ask if the rate includes linen—it usually does, but occasionally you will be required to supply your own sheets. Also, inquire about maid service; do you do the cleaning, or does the school?

8. Finally, ask about special rates for weekly or monthly vacations, and, of course, group rates where applicable.

HOSTELS ARE NOT ONLY FOR YOUTH. For one reason or another, most travellers believe that youth hostels limit their services to students. The fact is they serve people of every age. I travelled for years on the hostel route across Europe, and found them clean, comfortable, and the people hospitable. Often, the most interesting and energetic guests were those over the age of thirty.

There are more than four thousand youth hostels in forty-eight countries. They offer clean, well-run accommodations at incredibly low prices (under seven dollars a night usually) in almost any country you would consider travelling to, including the United States.

For a complete list of hostels, write to the American Youth Hostels Association, 20 West 17th Street, New York, New York 10011. Their affiliate, the International Youth Hostel Association, will accept your membership card. In London, the hostel association is quite well established, to the point of operating its own store for merchandise which hostel travellers will find useful all across the continent.

Another advantage of the hostel is the people. They are always friendly, and usually from all over the world. Hostels are an interesting place to meet a lot of interesting people, and to make new friends. Many times your vacation plans will change and become more complex because of the people you meet, the suggestions you hear, and the plans you make with hostel friends.

The accommodations at hostels vary greatly, but some have private rooms, some dormitories, many kitchen facilities and recreational facilities. You may find yourself lodging in a five hundred year old French chateau in a private chamber, or in a brand new Parisian university complex with swimming pool, tennis court, and outdoor track. Usually you are required to bring a sleeping bag or a sheet for your bed, but always the hostels provide their own bedding at a small extra fee.

THE YMCA AND YWCA. There are more than twenty-five hundred YWCA's and YMCA's around the world. They offer clean, well-maintained rooms with complete facilities including cafeterias, laundry services, phones, etc. They are often frequented by interesting travellers. All sponsor interesting and varied activities. The European counterpart of the American YWCA and YMCA has quite a different connotation than ours, in that it is not regarded as an impoverished substitute for hotel lodging. Many people prefer these associatons for lodging.

STUDENT HOUSING DISCOUNTS. There are a multitude of housing discounts for students, or for anyone in any vague way connected with education (try using your alumni card).

For example, the Empire Hotel near Lincoln

Center in New York City offers air-conditioned rooms with television and bath for half the price of their regular rate for the same rooms. This is less than you would pay anywhere in New York City for a decent hotel room. Similar savings are available in San Francisco and Los Angeles. In New York, contact the Council on International Education Exchange, Empire Hotel, Broadway and 65th Street, New York, New York. In San Francisco, contact the Hotel Stratford at 242 Powell Street, San Francisco, California. Always ask for the student rates at these establishments. In Los Angeles, call Northrop University Residence Halls, or write them at 733 Hindry Avenue, Inglewood, California. At some of these places you must share a bath, and at others you will get a private one. At all of them, breakfast is available, and often included in the price of the room, so be sure to get the specifics on what is available to you.

Another excellent move is to check with any local college or university when you arrive. Very often, they have special visiting student rates which are extremely low when compared to hotels. Just look in the phone book or ask around.

Also, send in for your Hilton Hotels and Inns discount card, good all over the United States. You'll get close to fifty percent off if you are a student, forty percent off if you are a faculty member, as long as the hotel is not expecting heavy bookings at the time you make the reservation. Write to Hilton Hotels, Fulfillment Department, 9880 Wilshire Boulevard, Beverly Hills, California.

RENT A HOUSE INSTEAD OF A ROOM. This section concerns itself with a totally new concept in vacation living, the house rental. The concept offers several advantages over hotel living.

Privacy. Most hotels are built to accommodate the largest number of people possible in the smallest reasonable space. Unfortunately, that means that even in luxury hotels you can practically be assured of hearing an occasional toilet flushing or a lovers' spat next door. What's worse, you are constantly surrounded by people. The lobby is filled, the dining room is jammed, the candy shop is crowded, and your one, single room is crowded, too, because you cannot just go off by yourself for a few minutes. You wouldn't think of living at home in one room, so why do it on vacation, especially if you have children.

Convenience. Although room service is nice, there is nothing like taking a cold beer out of your own refrigerator when you want it. Every traveller has had the experience of being told that the dining room doesn't open until 7 á.m. In spite of brochures to the contrary, the hotel makes you live by its rules. There is no need to do this if you rent a house.

Local life. If you live with the people, you get to know the language and customs even better. Many people truly enjoy learning about other people by travelling; while others would prefer to fly to an airport and be met by a stuffy tourguide who takes them to their room at the Hilton. Those who like the Hilton and tourguide will eat hamburgers from room service and buy Givenchy perfume at the hotel counter. One look at the Eiffel Tower tells them all they want to know about France.

Your purchase of this book, however, makes us positive that that's not your attitude. When you rent a house you do your own shopping at the local supermarket or grocery, just the the people do. You truely live among the people.

Price. Although houses come in all prices, there

are still heavy savings, especially when travelling with a family. The savings are not only in terms of room prices. Sure, it may be thirty-eight dollars a day instead of seventy-five, but you'll also save on everything from bellhop tips to food. After you've paid twenty dollars a few mornings in a row to feed your group breakfast at a hotel, maybe it's time to think about a house, and buying a few dollars in breakfast food at a local store.

Personally, I have found lovely little cottages, one in particular with two fireplaces, a private beach, three bedrooms, a living room, and a huge kitchen-meeting room all situated in the English countryside overlooking the sea, for eighty dollars a week. When you start thinking in terms of holidays outside of the cities, in the calm of the countryside of whatever country you are visiting, these jewels pop up frequently.

How to rent. There is a company that specializes in rental of apartments and villas throughout the world: Randalin Travel. They are located at 630 Lexington Avenue, New York City. It is very important to deal with a reputable company when renting a house. I have found myself stranded on the coast of Italy with no place to stay and no agent meeting me, because I did not fully check out the agency I was using. After all, you are taking property unseen for your whole vacation. The company we've suggested is publicly owned and specializes in this type of vacation. It will arrange to find you a property within your budget, and make sure it has utensils and bedding. It even has an agent pick you up at the airport. The rental includes a maid service, and for a slightly higher fee, you can get a full time maid and butler. In some countries, a cook and driver are also available at a slight fee.

One note of warning: If you decide to rent a house directly from an advertisement, be careful. You will need to be an expert in both the local language and the local law. Watch out, and know with whom you are dealing.

Here's a typical saving available by renting an apartment. Guam is a popular stopover point for Americans returning from the Far East. Hotel rooms go for upwards from $175 a night. Apartments go for as little as one fifth that price at the elegant Guam Towers per night (post office box 7080 R, Tamuning, Guam) and the shops are all duty free. Think about it!

CAMPING ABROAD. One inexpensive method of travelling is camping abroad. Your best bet is to write to the tourist offices of the countries you plan to visit to get the details. For complete up to the minute details on camping overseas, we recommend you contact: Motor Caravan Magazine, 67 Palfrey Heights, Brantham, Manningtree, Essex, Great Britain. Send two dollars for a sample copy; you'll find camping an interesting and inexpensive way to travel.

The rental of motorized campers has started to gain in popularity throughout Western Europe. Unfortunately, gasoline prices are higher than the United States, but you may save quite a bit in the long run because you won't be shelling out money for a hotel room. More and more caravan parks are being built all across the mountains and lovely scenic areas of European highlands.

Special hint: a camper-tour put together by Continental Campers, Inc., Post Office Box 7580 Schiphol Oost, Amsterdam, the Netherlands, is a super inexpensive tour in your own rental camper-van. If this kind of life appeals to you, write to them or talk to a Dutch KLM Airline representative because the package is too complex and valuable to squeeze into these few pages.

SAVINGS ON MEALS. The cost of eating abroad, especially in Northern and Western Europe, varies markedly with the traveler. All too often, cost has no relationship to the quality of food consumed. Furthermore, it is just as easy to get sick on food you paid ten dollars for as it is to become ill from a twenty-five cent snack. Here are several fairly obvious guidelines for saving on meals, and on health:

1. Water. In most European cities, and in the capital cities of most Westernized countries, tap water from the public system is safe from bacterial or other pollution. In Northern Europe, their water is probably safer than ours, and you will not get sick as long as you avoid taking water from wells or streams.

If you have any doubts about the water, and in the Far East, Near East, Africa, Central, and South American countries, you should, do not hesitate to drink only bottled water. When you are avoiding local water, do not use ice cubes made from local water, either.

Make sure that the bottled water is brought to your table completely sealed—many smaller restaurants try to save money by re-filling and re-sealing them.

2. Avoid high-priced, tourist-type restaurants. These are usually the ones advertised in magazines handed out at the airports. The food in such restaurants is not nearly of the caliber or authenticity as the smaller, less expensive ones, and so you have nothing to gain by patronizing them.

3. Avoid hotel food unless it is included in the cost

of your trip. Their food is usually mediocre and almost always overpriced. And because you are staying in the hotel and you see the workers there every day, you almost always feel obligated to tip higher than you would in a restaurant outside the hotel. This is unavoidable, it is merely a psychological fact. The way to avoid the situation, though, is to eat out as often as possible.

4. Think twice before you eat. Most of the time, stomach ailments during a trip are not really caused by the water or food lacking in quality, but from simple abuse of your body. Fatigue and excitement accompany any overseas vacation, as does over-eating. Too many Americans stuff themselves with two giant meals, a huge lunch European style and a huge dinner American style, and wash the food down with wine or beverages they don't drink normally, and then go running around shopping and sightseeing. What can you expect, other than a stomach ache?

5. Make sure that dairy products and meats were properly refrigerated. If you have any doubts, merely stick to things which cannot spoil, like boiled eggs, toast, etc.

6. Remember, the style of cooking may be very different from one which your stomach is used to. For example, in many Mediterranean countries, the heavy use of olive oil and tomatoes may be too much for you, so ask that your food be cooked in butter. Even in England, where you would expect a style of cooking similar to the American style, you will find that everything is fried, and after a couple of days of fried food, heavy with grease, your stomach will begin to complain. It may cost a little more to have foods prepared slightly different than the cooks would normally, but it's better than being

uncomfortable.

7. Do not eat any raw shellfish. You know even less about pollution in overseas beaches and inland waters than you do here.

8. Keep in mind the fact that you are in another country, and eating habits are different from those of the U.S. For example, Europeans rarely drink orange juice, so the supply is low and the cost often as high as two dollars a glass. On the other hand, they do get their vitamin C from grapefruit juice, which costs less than one tenth that of orange juice. Therefore, order grapefruit juice rather than orange juice. Another example is that in Paris, the crepe is quite cheap when bought from street vendors, and can be filled with your choice of sweet filling or cheese or meat filling, whereas in the United States, a crepe in a restaurant will often be quite expensive.

9. If you are travelling in Europe, buy a Michelin guide. These guides are put out by Europe's leading tire manufacturer, and list more than nine hundred restaurants in which you can get food cheaply.

10. If at all possible, obtain your own kitchen facilities and cook for yourself. Your experience in the United States should make it quite clear that it is cheaper to make your own meals than to eat out.

11. Take advantage of the savings offered through luncheon menus. Eat your big meal at around two-thirty or three p.m., and pay luncheon prices. Nine out of ten times you get the same quality, and size of serving that dinner customers receive, but at less than half the price.

12. Do what the locals do. In Europe, picnics are very popular. Do not ask your hotel to arrange one. Instead, go into a local supermarket, and without even knowing the language, pick out the foods you want and try them. You will be surprised at the

quality of the supermarkets in other parts of the world.

13. Contrary to the situation in the United States, foreign railroad stations usually have good food at reasonable prices.

14. American influence has caused numerous cafeterias and small restaurants to spring up all over the world. Prices are usually very reasonable, as is the food.

Generally, rest assured that cuisine is taken a lot more seriously overseas than it is in the United States, and that even the most modest of kitchens will be very attentive in the care they take in making your meal. And, they want and need your business, so you are not going to be poisoned by any decent restaurant.

TRAVELLER'S CHECKS. Everyone has heard of traveller's checks, but many people fail to realize that only certain ones are free.

The major traveller check companies charge a surcharge on the amount of checks you buy from them, pushing the cost of your checks past the bare amount you want. The best bet to get around this is Barclay's Traveller's Checks. They are free. And they are more widely accepted than Cook's checks (seventy-five cents per one hundred dollars in checks). Barclay's is one of the world's largest banks and provides this service, as well as others, for travellers.

We cannot emphasize enough the importance of carrying traveller's checks instead of personal checks or large amounts of cash. You are completely protected if your traveller's checks are stolen or lost, a protection you are not afforded if your personal checks or cash disappear. In addition to the protection afforded by traveller's checks, stop and remember the last time you tried to cash a personal check at an out of town location. Chances are you could not get your check cashed here in the United States. So, you can expect even more difficulty overseas.

All experienced travellers carry travellers checks. Without exception.

As far as cash is concerned, never carry more than you can actually afford to have stolen while on vacation. Instead, convert your travellers checks into handi-cash in the local currency as you need it.

INTERNATIONAL FREE CHECKING. This is the latest in free checking accounts, designed for the businessman who is continuously travelling through Europe and the Middle East. The only one we feel safe in recommending is Deak National Bank, Main Street, Fleischmanns, New York, which offers free checking with no minimum balance, no service charges, and no ledger fees. This account enables you to write checks in any world currency, and deposits can be mailed in from anywhere in the United States.

WHERE TO CHANGE YOUR CASH. One of the most frequent mistakes made by overseas travelers is waiting until they get to their destination before they change their dollars into the local money. With hard currencies, like the dollar, English pound sterling, West German mark, etc., you might as well wait until you get there. But with the so-called soft currencies, you may do a lot better making the cash switch in the United States before you go, or at the hotel you stay in, rather than the banks or official exchange outlets. In others, the banks are better than tourist-trap hotels. Don't be afraid to check the rates. Shop around as you would for anything else.

Why the difference? Many of the world's currencies are backed by weak economies. International bankers do not like to hold onto large amounts of them because one never knows when the money will be devalued against the hard currencies of the world. However, bank rates are set by the government of the foreign nations and must be complied with in the bank. The rates are not enforced at hotels and stores, nor are they enforced on international money houses like Perera's, in New York, and Deak and Company. In other words, currency of Argentina, Brazil, Colombia, Italy, Peru or Spain may be worth three times more officially than you can actually get for it in exchange at Perera's or Deak's. So you can BUY those currencies for less money at one of these agencies instead of at a bank, and you will make money on the deal. And on many of these currencies, there is no limit placed to the amount you can buy in the United States and take with you into that country, so if you buy here you will MAKE money on the deal. If the currency exchanges at three times the amount here than it does officially in its own country, then you will have three times the amount of money when you arrive there, or you will be able to purchase THREE TIMES AS MUCH.

To find other Foreign Money Brokers, simply check the Yellow Pages under the same title.

EXCHANGE RATES. These are the official exchange rates put out by the official accepted agency, usually Deak's or Perera's. Needless to say, revaluations of currency do occur periodically, so it is always best to check on the latest rates. To do this, ask your travel agent, banker, or call a money broker.

Several countries, such as Bulgaria,

Czechloslovakia, East Germany, Poland, Romania, Russia, and Yugoslavia, set up artificial exchange rates which are not backed up by relative economic strengths. In other words, the rate the government uses is designed to collect as many United States dollars as possible, which are then cashed in for even harder currencies.

Be sure to check with money brokers like Perrera's in an attempt to beat these official rates. Money is traded freely on world markets, often above or below the official rates, and you can often get better rates of exchange. But be sure of limits on currency you can take in with you.

NEED MONEY IN AN EMERGENCY? If you need money for an emergency while you are overseas, go directly to the nearest United States embassy or consulate and explain the problem. Embassy staffs are often able to arrange temporary international loans to tide you over, and occasionally maintain special funds designed for that specific purpose.

Another way of obtaining cash is to take advantage of the many overseas offices and outlets which accept American Express, or which are actual offices of the credit agency. In a matter of hours, funds can be cabled to you from the United States to anywhere in the world, except countries with which we have no business ties. Another protection is to carry credit cards with you. You will probably be surprised at the number of American cards honored throughout the world, and particularly in Europe and South America. Mastercharge and Visa are both widely honored. If you need cash in a hurry in Europe, you can make a withdrawal with your credit card, against your account. However, if your card is through a bank that does not have a branch in the city you are in, you will only be able to withdraw money at a particular, overall office for that credit card which you carry. So, before you leave be sure to check to maked sure that the bank of your credit card has offices in the cities you will be visiting, and if it doesn't, find the name and address from your credit card company of their overseas agents who can make bank drafts on your cards for you.

In any event, if you need money fast, go to the nearest pay phone and call the American embassy. If they cannot help you, hang up and call home (your family, relative, or friend) collect (it's much cheaper than a paid call). Tell whomever you speak to to go down to the nearest American Express office or Western Union Telegram outlet and wire you the money. When you do this, be sure to specify to which bank you want it wired—it does not matter what bank you choose as long as it is convenient to your location. All banks in Europe will accept money wires for people who are not their customers. But you must specify a particular bank and a particular branch of that bank, or the wire will arrive and it will sit on someone's desk for a week, will take another week to be processed and mailed to you, and in the meantime you are sitting around broke! And the money should arrive in a matter of hours, so the very next morning, before the bank notifies you, go directly to the branch you specified and ask if your money wire has arrived. Remember, when travelling overseas, you must always take the matters into your own hands. Never leave them to the bureaucracy to be taken care of.

If you are absolutely down and out, have not received your money wire, and cannot get drafts drawn on your credit cards, the absolute last resort is to go to a store and purchase something of the amount that you need, return it, and get the refund in cash.

One final note: stay away from any loans offered to you by foreign banks. The hassles are usually tremendous, and such loans should be an absolute last resort, unless recommended by the United States Embassy.

TIPPING. For some strange reason, tipping is an American problem. All other nationalities seem to know exactly who, how much, and when tipping comes into play, but Americans are either unsure, or just plain don't know. To compound the problem, and put holes in their wallets, Americans are always over-tipping. This is not only improper, but it is a definite insult in some countries. Believe it or not, to overtip is as wrong as to undertip.

Improper tipping practices can cost you more than one hundred dollars a week if you are not careful. The purpose of this section is to explain tipping procedures and amounts, and offers guidelines which even the professional traveller should review.

1. Always remember that tipping is for service. If the service is poor, ill-mannered, or in any way unsatisfactory, you should have no qualms about leaving no tip. The solution to rude cab drives and inattentive waiters is NOT a large tip to make them like you. The solution is not to try to win friends through giving money away, and they will just go and laugh at you after you leave. The solution is not to tip at all. Perhaps the next time they won't take their job for granted.

2. In many parts of the world, the required gratuity is included in your check or bill. Virtually every European hotel and restaurant, except in

Great Britain, Ireland, and Spain, includes a ten or fifteen percent service charge in your bill. Usually, you can find out whether the tip is included by a simple examination of the bill. Check the next to the last line. If you are still unsure, ask the manager. Don't ask the person who actually served you, because all too often they will lie.

In your hotel, the only persons you should tip before you leave are the porter who carries your baggage to your room, and the bellboy who delivers messages to you. All others wait until you are ready to leave, and then you settle with them.

Who should be tipped when you are ready to leave? Be sure to tip the concierge or hall porter at least twenty-five cents, and closer to one dollar if your stay has been more than three days. Or if his service has been special, as is so often the case with hall porters, because they can help with everything from giving you information about where to go and how to get there to finding you a car or a room in the next city of your vacation, tip him especially well for those services and you will be well treated on your return. In most foreign hotels, the porter who carried your bags also handled little extras like getting your shoes shined, and he should be tipped an additional twenty-five cents when you come in, and the same when you leave. Maids should always be tipped ten to fifteen percent a day, payable when you leave.

3. In restaurants, only tip if the service truly merits it. While you must pay the service charge, if any, included in the bill, you need not add anything to it unless you firmly believe you got what you like. If you are satisfied, an additional five percent is sufficient, to make a total of about fifteen percent. But too many waiters in expensive restaurants are

too used to large tips as well as a cut from the other charges as well as their pay, and their service may not really merit this. Do what you feel has integrity without regard for what others might think of you.

4. Be sure to tip washroom attendants. They get the smallest possible coin as a tip, unless a special service is performed. Usually, there is a plate near the door in foreign washrooms. If you have to pay for the use of the towel as well as the sink, do not tip. This is extortion.

5. IMPORTANT: Be sure to carry the smallest denominations of coins so you have the proper tip on hand. Most of those who would deserve tips know it, and deliberately do not carry change for larger coins and bills.

6. In France, you must tip the attendants at movie houses who point you to your seat. Usually a franc will suffice.

7. Tipping hairdressers varies depending on the quality level of the salon you are visiting. In medium priced salons, tip the washers one dollar and the dressers at least two dollars.

8. Learn the tipping customs in the country you are visiting. For example, people never tip in Fiji, Japan, and most Communist countries. On the other hand, in Russia, despite its communist economy, some servants expect you to leave a ten percent tip, while others refuse tips on grounds they are a capitalist custom. And, in Argentina, the average tip is twenty-two percent, well above the world average of fifteen percent.

9. The following people are never tipped: airline personnel, including counter clerks, pilots, stewardesses, and officers; ship captains and pursers; customs officials; immigration personnel; policemen (except in Mexico).

10. It is especially important for you to tip in the local currency when you are in a communist country, and usually a good policy in all others. Why? Because the people cannot readily, and are often completely forbidden by law, to cash in foreign money for their own brand. Hundreds of Russians risk stiff penalties to cash in American dollars on the Black Market; but, most Russians will not take the chance.

11. Do not tip because you feel pressured to do so; this is the surest way to lose your self-respect and to lose the respect, and thus get taken for a lot more money, of the servants around you.

12. In general, tip just like you would at home.

SAVINGS ON POSTAGE. One of the great joys of travelling is picture postcards and letters that go back to the folks in the United States. The length of your stay will determine how important these are. Yet, every year, thousands of Americans waste dozens of dollars on postage because they have not taken the time to learn how to mail items internationally, cheaply.

Here are some money-saving ideas/hints:

1. Invest in air letter sheets. Frequently you find on a post card that you have more to say than you can fit in the space. Do not write a letter. The air letter sheets are sheets of stationary which fold up and become pre-stamped, self-contained envelopes, and are available in almost every country in the world, including the United States. They are usually twenty to fifty percent less than regular air mail rates. For example, an air mail letter might cost you seventy-five cents to mail from Europe to the United States, yet as little as forty cents to mail an airmail letter sheet that contains as much information.

2. If you cannot obtain airmail sheets, or are

unable to fit everything you have to say onto one, then use tissue-weight letter paper to write your letters on. A traveller can easily waste ten dollars or more by using regular weight letter paper. Remember, letters fly by the ounce, and every sheet of paper of regular weight will weigh in at an ounce. Usually, when you buy air mail paper, the pad will be printed with the weight of several sheets folded together, so that you will know, even before you buy it, how much it will cost you to mail a letter of however many sheets to the United States.

3. Mail everything yourself. Most bellhops graciously offer to mail letters for you. At the time it may seem easier. You are rushing out to the bus and are late for a tour. Your bellhop or porter reaches his hand to your unstamped letter and offers to post it for you. It seems the logical thing to do. However, my experience has been that they often take your "airmail" letter and mail it at the cheaper, seamail rate, charging you for the airmail price. So make the short, interesting walk to the post office yourself; make time that afternoon as a relaxing walk, or the next morning before breakfast, but do it yourself.

STUDENT TRAVELLERS DISCOUNT CARD. I have devoted a separate section to this discount because of its tremendous value. The Council on International Education Exchange (CIEE) offers students an International Student ID card. It costs just a few dollars, is obtainable here or in Europe with a letter from your school stating you are a full-time student. Many times a student ID card from your college is sufficient proof of this. To obtain the card, go to your Student Travel Center at your university or college, or send the fee, along with proof, to CIEE, 777 United Nations Plaza, New York, New York, 10017.

NEWSPAPERS. People who normally buy a newspaper every day often do without them on vacations. This is a crucial error. Most major cities of the world have an English newspaper, including the Brazil Herald, the Bangkok Times, the Jerusalem Post, and the Paris Herald Tribune. It is important to buy the newspaper because you'll find a lot of timely local information which will vary with the newspaper, but you will always find news of local sports events, club meetings that may interest you, and a directory of additional English language newspapers.

In the Herald Tribune, for example, you will find the weather in major cities in the United States, for currency conversion rates, listings for European apartments to rent, and even a list of American churches throughout Europe. Also, the slant of the news in such a paper is from the American point of view. Often when you are travelling abroad the headlines and stories are from a completely different angle, and may distort the news from the manner you are used to receiving it. But an English language paper, usually American run, will present the news as you are used to reading it.

VIII.

HEALTH

Nothing can ruin a vacation more quickly than that sick feeling. The problem of missing out on all that planned vacation fun is compounded by the fact that good medical attention is all too often unavailable in many other countries.

The smart traveller uses preventitive medicine. He realizes that overseas travel is the classic situation in which an ounce of prevention is worth a pound (and in most foreign countries, a ton) of cure.

Some of the concepts that follow may seem basic, but we contend that most travellers who are affected are subject to carelessness, or failure to take the basic precautions.

1. Water. It may surprise some to learn that water is still very much a problem in many parts of the world. If you have even the slightest doubts, or if anyone has warned you of unsanitary conditions, or epidemic, do not drink the water. Remember, this rule includes ice cubes, too. All too often, travellers become ill from using ice cubes made from the local stuff in those fancy Polynesian drinks we all adore.

Fortunately, in most areas in which water on tap is a problem, they keep bottled water available for tourists. With bottled water you run into another problem. Many smaller restaurants try to save money any way they can; and, one way of doing this is to refill empty water jars out of the kitchen tap. What do you do? If you order bottled water, make sure you see your waiter/waitress open the bottle at your table. Ask specifically for this. It is better to be somewhat suspicious and demanding than somewhat nauseous and sick.

2. Be prepared. Before leaving home, pack a little kit of supplies. We recommend certain items because they may not be readily available if you need them when travelling. In addition, odds are that they will be very expensive in many other countries, and we do want to save our money for fun, not medicines.

Your kit should contain the following:

Vitamin C

Multiple Vitamins (which you should take every day)

Aspirin

Thermometer

Bandaids

Contac (or another anti-cold medicine)

Suntan lotion

Extra eyeglasses

Your eyeglass prescription

3. Avoid being overly naive. Sure, in New York you occasionally buy food from local street vendors, but you can keep track of who they are because they are clearly licensed. And yes, you do sample ethnic dishes from sidewalk stands here in the United States. But what about that mini-taco stand in the bus station in Acapulco? You're hungry from a late awakening and no breakfast, your bus to the site is leaving...don't eat that taco! When you go overseas

you have to remember that you are not in the United States, and that thousands of travellers become ill every year from bad food.

Usually food in Germany, France, and Scandinavian countries is fresh and well-prepared. However, beware of Italy, Spain, England, all Latin American countries, and definitely all Middle Eastern and North African countries.

Sure, you should eat the local food, but pass up the sidewalk food. Also, unless you are absolutely crazy about pork, and perhaps, just plain absolutely crazy, avoid pork like the plague. In the United States, pork products are closely regulated, but the same can rarely be said for other nations.

4. If you are sick, get help quickly when you need it. This is a travel guide designed to save you money but as the Bible says, life comes before all else. We strongly suggest that you not save money in the area of medical attention. If you feel you might want to see a doctor while travelling, ask some other American travellers staying with you, or ask the local police or American Consul, for a doctor. The best place to find an English-speaking doctor is usually at the big hotels, American Embassy, or the British Embassy.

Always, if possible, go to American or British hospitals. This is not imperialistic hogwash: American and British doctors are always the best, and the most well-educated in recent techniques. In Paris, or anywhere near Paris, go to the American Hospital at Neuilly.

In Britain, you will not be charged except a minimal fee for the services which are rendered you.

5. In general, take it easy. You are on vacation. You are supposed to relax, so do so. Americans make travelling hard business, oftentimes. Do not

set a certain amount of miles you feel you have to cover, this leads to over-exertion and exhaustion and illness. When you arrive at your destination, resist that urge to jump right off your flight and begin sight-seeing. Instead, go to your hotel and relax. Eat dinner nearby, and get a good night's sleep that first evening. You'll feel better for it.

6. Watch out for surgery. Most surgical conditions can wait twenty-four hours. It is almost always a bad move to undergo surgery abroad. Most hospitals are not well-enough equipped with emergency measures in hospitals abroad to handle situations the way American hospitals are, except of course, the American hospitals. In case of an emergency, ask the doctor if the condition will be aggravated by a few hours. If the answer is "no," get on the next flight back to the United States. The American Embassy can be very helpful in getting the sick person an immediate flight home.

IX

COMMUNICATING:
or Making Yourself Heard

LANGUAGE LESSONS ON A BUDGET. To really enjoy the country you are visiting, you should know the language. Although today many of the world's schools teach everyone English, it is still important to speak a man's language to get to know him. One of the most enjoyable things on a trip is to really converse with a native. Unfortunately, the language courses in American high schools are frequently poor. We know of only one person who can fluently speak Spanish based on high school lessons only. Most of our friends are merely able to repeat a few isolated words and phrases, and conjugate verbs. No one wants to hear you say, "Peter is leaving for school." Nor are they interested in hearing you conjugate the verb "to be".

· The time has come for a real traveller to speak a foreign language. Unfortunately, the courses at Berlitz-type places are expensive. In addition, you only know a language from constant use. Therefore, our suggestion is to really get in there and learn the language.

The best way to do this is to prepare for your trip a few months in advance, by placing an advertisement in the International newspapers, the local university newspapers, or by contacting your local International Student Center. The ad should read something like the one below:

> "American student from _____
> University will tutor English in
> exchange for Spanish lessons.
> Wants to live with Spanish family
> this summer."

In this way you will get to use your language constantly. If you have the time, you might consider learning the language in the foreign country itself. In which case, add the following lines to your advertisement:

> "Will pay room and board. Write:
>
> _____ "

You will be surprised at the number of replies you will get, and the low price of classified ads.

If you do not have the time or the inclination to learn a foreign language, at least learn the basic words for the basic exchanges which can be found in any travel phrase book. Do not buy the book at the airport the day before you leave. To leave the study until this late date is a grand mistake, for these phrasebooks are not written for immediate study. You must take at least two weeks to learn the pronunciation and use of the different basic phrases. There is no better way to throw your money away, than to appear as though you haven't the slightest glimpse of what the foreign words mean. If you were a taxi driver and a Japanese man got into your car and handed you a wad of money and asked you "how much?" in Japanese, would you give him nine hundred and ninety dollars change for a ten dollar ride? Or would you keep a large portion of it for yourself?

English is sufficient to get you by in several countries, although in all cases, it is truly "getting by" and no more. If you want to learn about the people and their customs, you must put yourself out a bit to learn a few of their phrases. In the following countries, though, English will be sufficient: Ireland, Belgium, Israel, England, Scotland, Holland, Denmark, Norway, Germany, Switzerland, Sweden, Luxembourg, South Africa, Egypt, Hong Kong, Mexico and most of the South and Central America, Canada, Japan, Taiwan, Russia (cities only), Australia, New Zealand, Phillipines, Jordan. You will not feel at home in these countries with only English; you will feel like a foreigner. If you spend just a little of bit of time to learn a few phrases, however, your vacation experience will be greatly heightened.

French will help in the following countries:

France, the Middle East and North Africa, French Canada, Tropical Africa, Italy, and Spain.

X

SETTLING IN
or Working and Living Away From Home

LIVING ABROAD. We have all heard stories of an American businessman who has his company transfer him to Europe. He then banks his salary and lives on his expense account plus about twelve cents per week in cash. Alas, the story is no longer true. Prices in the world's large cities are fast becoming a parity situation. In fact, it is more expensive to live in Paris than in New York. Many people marvel at the cost of thirty-five dollars for dinner in a low-class New York restaurant. Yet few know that in Tokyo the price is four times as much.

But before this chapter totally discourages you, there are some facts you should know. First is that many outer regions in Europe are inexpensive. Second, the pace in many other parts of the world is slower. Third, if you live like the natives do, you will always be able to get by: after all, they do, don't they?

If you want to live out of the country look to many different places than just Europe. For example, you may find the climate, living conditions, and work situation nicer in Haiti than in France. A close friend of mine, a labor lawyer, a few years ago grew fed up with California politics, and began looking around for a restful, interesting spot to move his practice and his family. In the end he opted for Samoa—Pago Pago, because it is American-owned and thus he could still practice law, and yet it is a completely different culture. And because it is American, he didn't even have to learn a different language!

Take Haiti as an example. You should never let superficial political situations scare you off. In Haiti conditions are not favorable if you are Hàitian. However, the government wants to attract Americans so they go out of their way to be kind to Americans settling there. Special allowances are made, even special tax situations are sometimes worked out. Skilled people, and people with businesses to establish there, are always welcome and encouraged. The reverse, though, is true in many European countries.

A starting point is to talk to other Americans that have settled in a place rather than talking to natives. Also, a visit to the American Embassy will prove useful.

To get a real feel for opportunities that a country can offer you, there is a special program in Putney, Vermont called THE EXPERIMENT, whereby you will have the opportunity to live with a family abroad for two or three months. This group is non-profit and can also help you with travel arrangements. This trial run should prove most worthwhile. Even if you don't go through this organization, an extensive visit to the country of your choice is essential. Extensive, by the way, means more than two weeks or even one month in a city. It means living in one place and not travelling from hotel to hotel; it means going alone and trying to make friends among the natives. All of these things are essential to seeing if you can or want to live in that country.

Another plan to really get you into the country is the Home Exchange Plan by which you actually trade homes (or apartments) with someone from overseas. For details, write The Vacation Exchange Club, 350 Broadway, New York, New York.

If you are really serious about moving to another country, for your next vacation, try out your plan to live abroad by renting a house (instead of a hotel room) and living like the natives. Shop at supermarkets instead of using room service and go by subway, not car or taxi. In short, live as you would if you were overseas. To obtain an apartment anywhere in the world, call or write Randalin Travel, 630 Lexington Avenue, New York, New York. This company has listings of over ten thousand houses and apartments in hundreds of countries. They rent these houses for a week, a month, or a year.

When you have definitely decided to move, and you have experimented for a few months with living abroad, make your move and enjoy it, but remember there must be a long period of adjustment. It will take you at least three months to settle in, to get used to everything having different names (even in English-speaking countries), and to make friends. You will be alone much of the time. In such a situation, you must make an intense effort to be social; you must try every day to meet new people and always be interested in what is happening on the street around you. This is an intense learning situation: be open to all sorts of new input and new customs.

EMPLOYMENT OVERSEAS. Woe unto the American who hopes to land a job overseas and work his or her way through a few months in Europe, the Far East, Africa, etc. Jobs are few and far between, salaries are generally insufficient to allow one to survive comfortably, and barriers continue to spring up every word in terms of immigration laws being passed.

Seventy percent of college graduates have such a goal in mind, and fewer than five percent are able to realize it. The statistics are definitely not with you. The work that you usually will find is cheap labor, maid service, waitressing; it is generally illegally obtained, and you will be in constant fear of being deported. And remember, once deported, it will be very difficult for you ever to return to the country, even for a visit.

If you are undaunted by such talk, let me next say that only a certain personality type will ever have a chance of obtaining a job abroad. Introverts are simply not impressive enough, no matter how good they are as ethical people, to immediately convince a foreign employer that they should risk heavy fines to hire you. You must be fast-talking, not only in your language, but also in theirs, and you must have some immediately marketable skill: teaching, (that's English as a Foreign Language, not math or American history), carpentry, cooking (as a chef), or waitressing.

The first problem would-be workers run into is that of obtaining an international work permit. This is very near to an impossibility unless you already have an employer in the country you plan to visit. More and more countries are following the British example of routinely questioning entrants into their country to weed out potential welfare cases and labor law violations (sometimes you can get jobs at below minimum wage.)

Your second obstacle is language. Unless you speak the local tongue fluently, forget about working in non-English speaking countries. And, if you cannot write the other language fluently, forget about anything other than the most menial of employments.

Next, consider the reactions of Americans to "cheap" foreign labor imported into the United States to undercut unions. Well, Europeans echo those very same feelings when Asiatics, Africans, and would-be sightseeing Americans who are willing to work for sub-union wages, do the same thing over there. Self-employment is difficult because of the incredible number of licenses required by the United States governments as well.

Even if you do qualify as self-employed, if you set up residence in another country, most only allow you to stay (unless you are a student) for a few months. You must have your passport stamped every three to six months with a new visa, which requires you exiting and re-entering their country each time, and this can end up being more trouble than it's worth.

If you do manage to discover a possible job, take a realistic look at what you are getting into. Many times you will be misled by companies offering salaries at which you can "live comfortably" the European or local way. But, the European and local ways are often the equivalent of lower class or poverty levels in the United States. Find out the equivalency rating of your European weekly salary and see what its buying power would be in dollars.

Then, go to a travel agent and ask him if a person you know who is living in that country is really living in luxury, as the advertisement claims. Chances are, it's not American luxury, that's for sure!

In general, travellers are much better off staying home and working in the United States, saving their money in anticipation of a trip overseas, and thus, really being free to enjoy their vacation. However, there are some very good job opportunities overseas. The odds of finding one are about one in a thousand, but if that one chance should come your way, jump on it. We've already begun explaining the way to find out if the promised job is really all it's made out to be, so now we'll move on to the best methods for obtaining overseas employment.

If you are a college student, consult your local advisor. There are special programs for you, it may involve menial jobs in hotels or university residences, but you will be living and working in a foreign country, and legally at that. Chances are your advisor has several job listings in other countries, particularly in the scientific and business areas. Always ask if anyone has taken the job(s) before, and what that person said about the job upon his or her return.

Your next best sources are the Council on International Education Exchange, 777 United Nations Plaza, New York, New York. Not only can you obtain an international student identification card through this organization, but it will also help steer you on the right track to reasonable jobs.

Several travel guides report that a new organization, the American Student Information Service (22 avenue de la Liberte, Luxembourg) lists more than one thousand summer jobs open to

American students seeking overseas summer employment. You must apply for membership, and if your application is accepted, you will be assigned to a job, usually a menial one, according to the guides. My attempts to contact the organization have gone unanswered so far...but sometimes international mails take months.

Another, more straight-forward alternative are international work camps, which offer lodging, meals, and a miniscule salary in exchange for employment in conservation work, teaching, or technical areas. Your best bet is to contact The American Friends Service Committee, 160 North Fifteenth Street, Philadelphia, Pennsylvania, or the Coordinating Committee for International Voluntary Service, UNESCO, 1 rue Miollis, Paris, France.

Another strong move for a good overseas job is to contact the airlines, government embassies, and universities of the country you desire to work in. In some cases, fine jobs turn up. We know of a young lady who worked with a German University as an English teacher, summer only, and made more than two thousand dollars, but that is a rare exception to the general rule.

If you don't mind working for the army, without actually joining of course, there are several possibilities in this regard. You can contact the University of Maryland, Army Educational Department, and explain that you are interested in teaching abroad at one of their bases. In this situation, you will be assigned to an American school for the children of Army personnel overseas. In most cases you will end up in West Germany, which is an excellent base for seeing the rest of Europe.

If you aren't qualified as a teacher, there are also other possibilities with the Army. They need all sorts of clerical positions filled which they don't fill with their own personnel. Contact the Employment office of the Army in Bonn, Germany, and ask for details about openings.

If you are interested in working in London, or any large English city, there are many possibilities for temporary office help, skilled and unskilled. If you can type, or even if you just want to work as a file clerk, you will be paid a living wage at many of the temporary agencies across the country. This is quite legal at this point in time, because the immigration laws pertaining to temporary workers in England are so ambiguous now that no one questions who can work and who cannot. Consequently, temporary agencies take the visa stamp on your passport, as long as it does not say you CANNOT work, as permission to work temporarily. A good bet for finding quick work is to check into any of the many Australian temp agencies in London, which are used to hiring Australian, Canadian, and New Zealand travelling people, and who will not be adverse to hiring Americans without specific work permits temporarily.

XI

SHOPPING

Americans travelling abroad have long been a fascination to natives. There are innumerable stories of people who have worked fifty weeks a year to go on a two-week vacation, spend more than two thousand dollars on airline tickets and hotel rooms, and then waste half of their time trudging through horrible sections of foreign cities just to save a few dollars on a sweater or a painting.

The incredible fact is that bargain hunting is the favorite pasttime of American tourists. The unfortunate fact is that, with the devaluation of the American dollar, coupled with the phenomenal increase in tourism abroad, the "bargains" which used to exist in the fifties have frequently diminished or disappeared.

However, there are some ways to bargain shop and come home with incredibly fantastic finds. One of these is the flea market. It is simply an open-air market to which dealers and residents of an area bring every conceivable kind of product to a central area to sell to natives and tourists. You will often discover antiques, second-hand furniture, invaluable junk from basements, produce grown locally, and a collection of buys that have been brought in from Japan to trick tourists. However, if you are careful, you can make yourself some money. I once paid eight francs, then about two dollars, in the Parisian flea market at Porte de Vincennes, for a twenty page, "uncollected" pamphlet publication of a short story by the American writer, J.D. Salinger. The French shopkeeper apparently had no idea who this writer was, or that his "uncollected" works might be valuable. When I got back to New York, I had the pamphlet appraised by a rare book dealer: valued at ninety dollars, for a twenty page pamphlet!

Frequently a flea market is a full-day, or several days' work and fun. This is one type of bargain shopping which is both interesting and rewarding. Tucked away in corners of the world's flea markets you are bound to find undiscovered treasures.

Another personal example: after trudging through a French flea market for an entire day, when almost ready to give up and go back to my hotel, we encountered an older man with his wares spread upon a blanket. He was selling a leather box which was attractive to the eye. We opened the box, and found a collection of jewelry inside. Most of it costume pieces and junk, but there were five early silver pieces from nineteenth century France. The price for the entire box was less than two dollars in American money, the coins alone were worth more than fifty dollars.

Admittedly, this was a rare find. However, you, too, can make so-called rare finds in collections of odds and ends which often hide valuable items. Just stop and consider the origin of the term "flea market". It comes from the tenth century, when trading spots were where these types of gatherings began. Rag pickers would often show up with their wares, and upon shaking them out, a buyer would usually find them covered with fleas or flea holes. But sometimes the buyer would find some perfect pieces in with the infested ones.

There are currently hundreds of markets in Europe alone, and these house thousands of dealers. This chapter is far from a complete directory, but by asking around in your destination, you will easily supplement it.

In London, check out the Petticoat Lane Market, open Sundays from 9 a.m. Simply take a cab from your hotel to Middlesex Street, in the eastern section of the city. Board the subway and ride to Liverpool Street on the Central, Circle, or Metropolitan Lines. At this market, you will find many dealers and stalls, housing all kinds of products ranging from antiques and pewter to produce and fish and chips. Another stop for shoppers is the Portobello Road market, staged every Saturday. Just tell your driver to take you to Portobello Road and put on your walking shoes. The market extends for miles, and is supplemented by dozens of antique stores. Best buys here are usually jewelry, antiques, bric a brac, books and weapons. You can also take the District-Circle Line to Notting Hill Gate, exit and walk down Pembridge Road. At the top of the road, and good to know about after you have spent a long, warm day of walking up and down the lane, is a splendid pub, called the Sun in Splendor. Another specialty of Portobello Road are the map and print shops, dealing in antique maps and prints as well as modern ones, all run by crotchety old, interesting English people.

The world's finest flea market is in Paris. It is a community in itself, an entire experience of French life, and a place which is not on the main tour guides. It is located at the Porte de Clignancourt. It is open every Saturday, Sunday, and Monday for the entire day, and spreads out in every direction. Bargaining is the key here. If your French is poor, carry a pad and pencil on which you write a price, and then wait for a counter-offer. The best time to hit this market is late Monday night, when everyone is packing up and merely trying to unload leftovers which were over-priced during the weekend's spree. You can find ANYTHING you want here, new or old, from jewelry to furniture to lunch, to musical instruments, to clothing. Wonderful costumery and hats. French film stars. Even an old-style French cabaret is housed within the acres of flea market here. Particularly enchanting, were the North African imports, the like of which I have not seen since I was in Morocco, beautiful embroidery and silk and satin dresses, caftans, and galabeahs.

The following is a list of other flea markets with good reputations for outstanding values. Ask locally for directions:

Porte de Vincinnes, Paris
Swiss Village, Paris
Porte de Montreiul, Paris
Place d'Aligre, Paris
Hamburg Flea Market, West Germany
Munich Flea Market, West Germany
Turin Flea Market, Italy
Bologna Flea Market, Italy
Florence Flea Market, Italy
Milano Flea Market, Italy
Via Portuenze Flea Market, Rome
Piazza de Fontanalla Borghese Flea Market, Rome

RATING THE EUROPEAN PRICES. The purpose of this section is to list the Europeans in order of cost, from the most expensive nations (Scandinavian) to the least expensive (Greece, Turkey, Poland, and Bulgaria).

If budgeting is a real concern, stay away from Sweden, Switzerland and Norway except for the scenery, because they are the three most expensive countries on the continent. Denmark and West Germany are not far behind in the battle for the greatest expense to the traveller. You know when you pay literally five dollars for a cup of regular coffee in Sweden, that to buy anything else, a scarf, a sweater, a bottle of perfume, is going to be exorbitant.

Austria, Belgium, and the Netherlands offer better opportunities to save a buck, and Finland is substantially less expensive and considered quite reasonable by most people.

Great Britain and France range from as expensive as anywhere in the world, downtown London and Paris that is, to as inexpensive as anywhere in Western Europe, if you know where to shop. A hint about buying wool products in England and Scotland: I have found a shop in London, Westaway and Westaway, across the street from the British Museum, where I find I can buy any kind of knitted wool product, in beautiful colors and excellent quality, cheaper than it can be bought in the countryside, or even in Scotland itself, where these products are made. The prices are absolutely unbeatable, as is the quality of the woolens. And frequently, you can find special sales in the sale shop (there are five different shops along the same street, all run by the same company under the same name, each specializing in a different aspect of wool products), that are truly incredible. I have purchased cashmere scarves and sweaters in that sale shop for under two dollars (the scarves) and under fifteen dollars (the sweaters). My favorite find was a brilliant red winter shawl, pure mohair, for five dollars. If you are in the market for such bargains and products, this shop is not to be missed.

In Paris, for good bargains, try the tiny stores in the fifth and sixth arrondisements. Many of them are run by young, small businessmen, who have not acquired the big city marketing sense yet, and charge lesser prices for items which might be very expensive in other parts of town.

Compared to the northern countries, Italy is less expensive, but slowly joining the upward trend. Italy has recently become the fashion capital of the world, and is no longer the place to buy fashion bargains. For the latest in trends, and expensive, chic clothes, it is terrific, but for saving money, skip Italy when it comes to clothes.

The real bargains in Western Europe are Spain and Portugal, where leather goods, including fashion boots and beautiful, hand-carved leather bags, are still quite inexpensive.

Greece, Morocco, and Turkey are dirt cheap, as are Poland and Bulgaria. The other Communist countries vary in prices, as does Yugoslavia. We recommend that you stay out of Albania: the government is hostile to Americans, and so are its prices!

Basically, the bargains available while travelling are innumerable. They are usually obtained by shopping less heavily travelled tourist regions, and the farther one gets into the country and out of the city, the greater the potential for super bargains. Of course, the worst place to make any purchases are the hotel gift shops. These are usually establishments run by the hotel with owner mark-ups of four and five times! But if you concentrate your buying in the countryside, you will do well. A carved figurine from West Germany can be purchased in Munich or Bavaria for forty dollars, and the same figurine can be purchased in the countryside from whence it comes in Oberammergau for twenty-five. And if you want to go to one of the smaller, less tourist-infested towns in the same area as Oberammergau, you can pick up that same figurine for fifteen! So by taking a lovely train trip to a quaint little mountain town, by talking to the Bavarian people and learning a little about what they live for, you can save yourself twenty-five dollars!

Duty-free shops are the place to buy tobacco, liquor, and perfumes. Any products which are heavily taxed can be purchased at substantial savings at the duty-free shop. This is also true when bringing products into the country. For example, before you leave from New York going to Europe, you can purchase cigarettes at a duty-free shop for less than four dollars a carton.

In Europe, a pack of cigarettes usually costs $1.20

to 2.00. However, bear in mind that purchases from duty-free shops are frequently delivered on the plane. Therefore, if you are travelling from London to New York, and your duty-free purchase is four quarts of liquor, you may save a few dollars, but you will have the tremendous discomfort of travelling with these large and bulky packages under your legs. Airline personnel sometimes will hold purchases for you, but at other times, they will not.

A special note here about what not to buy. It's important to remember that the laws in other countries are not only more severe than American laws, but more severely regulated. Frequently, American tourists have made the tragic mistake of attempting to make fabulous bargain purchases of illegal drugs like hashish and marijuana. A word to the wise: these drugs carry tremendous penalties if you are captured in customs. But, more importantly, if you are captured in the country in which they are sold, a long jail sentence will await you, and the American government can do little to help you. One friend of mine was in prison in Spain for three years before he feigned insanity in order to be released, because the legal process offered him absolutely no hope. There are countless other stories of Americans who are now jailed for terms of up to twenty years for dealing drugs in countries like Spain and Portugal. Worst of all, the American Embassy has its hands tied, and foreign prisons make ours look like plush penthouses.

Therefore, while you are looking for bargains, one thing to stay away from is bargains in drugs. The fact is that the drug bargain hunters are invariably caught, often because the person who sold you the drugs is a government agent, or a dealer who will turn you in to the authorities to earn a reward, thereby significantly increasing his profit. We repeat an important message which is stated in various handbooks issued by the United States government:

"Avoid the temptation to deal in anything illegal while outside of the United States."

In these times, when it is so fashionable to talk about the loss of freedom in America, all one has to do is visit the courts of any foreign country and you will suddenly realize how lucky we are here. We are not trying to be political, but rather to give a guideline on one special kind of bargain to avoid.

It is also important to know your seller. Of course, a charming little pottery vase bought in a small town outside of Mexico City for eight cents holds little potential problem for the purchaser. However if you are shopping for silver and diamonds, or fine products, make sure that you either know the product that you are buying or that you know the person from whom you are buying it. Unfortunately, many businesses, especially those in smaller cities, prey upon American tourists who are looking for bargains to bring home.

One final note. Before you leave, register with the United States customs any foreign-made products you are carrying with you, such as your Swiss-made watch, your Japanese camera and your English walking stick. Hold onto this registration receipt, because if you are not careful, you will wind up paying duty on these items again. I constantly carry a typewriter that was made in Barcelona. It is ten years old and looks it, yet the last time I returned to the United States from England, and not having been to Spain on that trip at all, a customs man took an instant dislike to me and decided that he would challenge my typewriter as a new purchase. I had to pay duty on it again, after ten years interim period. And there is nothing you can do to protest. The customs men are gods; what they decide is final, and if you protest they will only make it more difficult for you. So save yourself problems, and possibly money, and register everything that is foreign made that you take with you.

And, speaking of duty, you can mail packages back to the United States to friends and avoid paying duty. This is done simply by taking the package to the Post Office, marking it Parcel Post and clearly putting on the package the word "Gift value under ten dollars". You can send an unlimited number of packages into the United States from abroad as long as they are gifts with retail value under ten dollars.

PHOTOGRAPHY BARGAINS. If you've visited your local camera store lately, or gone out pricing cameras as gifts, you know that the cost of cameras, film, and developing has skyrocketed. Too often, American travellers buy expensive cameras in the United States in anticipation of the great photographs they will take overseas, only to come home greatly disappointed by bad weather, or the wrong film. Make sure the film you buy will be right for what you want to shoot. If you plan on taking action shots, be sure to purchase some "fast" film; if you will only go for "stills", save some money and buy regular film. And remember, if you buy a new expensive camera specifically for a trip abroad, give yourself plenty of time to practice with the camera and to get used to it before you leave, so you don't come home with overexposed or underexposed photographs of all those beautiful scenes.

If you plan to buy a camera for your trip, it is often a good idea to buy the camera when you are overseas. You can save as much as fifty percent by buying it in a duty-free shop. You can also purchase 35mm film in bulk, and then wind it onto your spools yourself. You save up to sixty percent!

You should also take care to have your film developed by a reputable film processor-developer, and can save a lot of money by having it processed in the United States. Film processors in England and France are exorbitantly expensive, so never have your film developed there. Photo-finishers are very expensive overseas; you can save upwards of fifty percent by using mail photo-finishers. Beacon Photo Service, Rockville Center, New York, has proved to be very reliable. Just send a stamped, self-addressed envelope and they'll send you a free film processing envelope and prices.

One other note: if you mail your film home for processing, mark it clearly with the following legend: ATTENTION POSTMAST & CUSTOMS: FILMS FOR DEVELOPING ENCLOSED, EXAMINE WITH CARE.

BARGAINS AT AUCTIONS. If you are interested in better grade values, and there are no duties on antiques, the world's greatest auction room should be your oyster.

In England: Sotheby; Christie;
          Manson & Woods
In Bern: Klipstein and Kornfeld
In Vienna: Dorotheum
In Paris: Hotel Drouot

The rules for bargain-hunting are pretty much the same as in the United States. That is, the bargains are there as long as you don't get caught up in the wild bidding. These become even more of a challenge when the bidding is ⸳ ⸳reign currency. But, if you are willing to work at ⸳ ⸳ the values are there.

Most auction houses have merchandise on display before the sale. Certainly inspect it so you can discover flaws and true worth. Set an idea of how much you are willing to pay, and don't go over it. And one final tip: never make the first bid, let someone else set the starting point. You may wind up buying it cheaper that way.

THE MAN WITH A DEAL. Everyone is looking for bargains, and we all come across street vendors sooner or later. They are usually the kindest looking souls, frequently impoverished, full of tearful stories or comic tales, but watch out for them!

With the exception of sellers at flea markets, street sellers are frequently unreliable, and often "slightly less than honest." Their prices are invariably invitingly low, but in most cases, so is the quality of their merchandise.

The usual "shovelfull" is that their overhead is very low, or they deal in tremendous volume. We have stories of gold watches which turned out to be tin; of fine perfumes that were counterfeit labels on junky toilet water; and of course, a buy on a special precious stone which turned out to be a rock. Know your seller or know your merchandise. And if you know your merchandise, watch out for the old "switcheroo". Not too long ago, we met a young fellow who was rather sad. He had sampled some fine tea and made a purchase at what he believed were bargain prices. His purchase turned out to be ground seaweed. The seller had pulled the old "switcheroo" and then disappeared into the hills, or got back on his boat to fish for some more "tea".

WILL I GET RIPPED OFF? We'll probably get

beseiged by angry members of one ethnic group or another for including a list like this, but this book is written for you, the traveller, and is supposed to save you money.

Our object is to save money wherever possible. One way to lose money quickly is to fall for all of the unsuspecting tourist gags and tricks which occur in all parts of the world. The typical move is the taxi driver who "did not understand where you wanted to go" and went to the wrong place. Now, he doesn't speak no English, mahn, so you cannot even explain the mistake. What's more, he has no and all you've got are large bills.

Another street trick: "Bargains" on jewelry. Always be suspicious of any offers of cut rates. Odds are it's a fake designed to lure the unsuspecting customer.

Simply put, here is a list of the odds of getting ripped off in purchases and services in the countries we've frequented:

Country	0/0
Switzerland	2
USSR	8
Holland	9
Japan	11
Scandinavia	15
Britain	15
Ireland	15
Eastern Europe	15-20
New Zealand	17
South Africa	17
Australia	18
West Germany	21

Country	0/0
Spain	23
Portugal	23
Hungary	25
Greece	28
Iran	30
North Africa	35
Austria	38
Philippines	40
Hong Kong	45
Italy	60
France	75

Tropical Africa, Canada and Taiwan are not rated, but we have had fairly good experiences there. Syria, Iraq, Saudi Arabia, the United Arab Emirates are big rip-offs. Good buys can be had in Egypt, Jordan, and Israel if you know your merchandise, and are a pro at the art of haggling. South American and Central American countries are rip-off paradises, but not as bad as France.

LOCK IT UP. This book is designed to save you money. It goes without saying to be sure to hold onto what you have, and what you purchase. Crime is not just an American problem. It's world-wide in scope, and worse overseas than here. In poorer countries, even the crooks know that it's the tourists who have the cash. To protect yourself, always lock valuables in the hotel safe, and save your receipt. Invest in a travel lock; they cost about ten dollars and are available in any hardware store. Do not turn in your hotel keys. Pop them into the mail when you leave. That way, you have no fears of someone picking up that fine ring you forgot. Also, do not turn in your key when you leave the hotel for a day of sightseeing. If you return and find something missing, notify the hotel and call the police. Get the number of the police report; you'll need this to file your insurance claim. Get baggage and effects insurance if you are travelling with goods of real value to you. It is usually very cheap—under a dollar for one hundred dollar value, and protect your goods on land and in the air.

WHERE NOT TO SHOP. Now that we have discussed the places where to go for good bargains, let me take a few lines to tell you the places absolutely to avoid for shopping.

1. The Eiffel Tower-like spreads. These are the blanket spreads in front of every tourist location across Europe, from the Eiffel Tower to Trafalgar Square to the Venice Canal docks. They are operated by large chains, large conglomerates, and the same merchandise is for sale in each of these countries, at each of these spreads. It may look like authentically carved Moroccan leather to you, but rest assured that it is not. You will be harrassed and called out at if you walk by these places without stopping, but nevertheless, the merchandise is worth nothing.

2. Although one of the finest stores in the world is Harrod's Department Store in London, and although you should certainly visit it to see luxury at its optimum, and to see a store where anything is obtainable, whatever is for sale at Harrod's is obtainable elsewhere for less. Harrod's caters to the rich in London and the rich tourist, to the Arab sheik and the Italian prince. If you are saving money, do not buy an umbrella here, nor yarn, nor food in their luxurious food halls. Everything is vastly overpriced.

3. Never shop at the rue de Rivoli in Paris, for while it is one of the most beautiful streets in the world, it is also one of the most expensive, priced exclusively for the tourists.

4. Never shop at hotel gift shops.

5. Above all, unless you know exactly what you want and how much you want to spend on it, never buy anything on the first day of your trip. Many people are often overcome at being in a foreign country, and begin to buy things the minute they arrive. This is a gross error in judgment, as you are bound to see the same items in many different places throughout your trip. I once bought a lovely statue in Mexico City which I thought was a bargain, yet in Merida I saw the entire set of statues for the same price as the one I paid in Mexico City.

It is also a good idea to wait to the end of your trip to buy extensively, because that way you won't have to carry bags and bags of purchases from country to country. If you have rented a car, this is not such a great problem, but if you are travelling by train, or by plane, making those connections will be a great problem, and you may even end up leaving some of your purchases at some anonymous train station, because it was just too much trouble to tote them one more time.

XII

BUDGET YOURSELF

One of the best ways, amazing as it may seem, to save money, is the pencil and budget method. This is simply accomplished by preplanning a budget for your trip. Then while vacationing, write down every important expenditure before you make it. This forces you to see if the expense you are about to incur is really within your budget, and the slight effort required in writing it down will make you reconsider the importance of the expenditure.

It's always important to remember that while you are travelling, you are constantly spending money. Every day you will dribble away a few dollars on a drink you really didn't want or need, an extra cab ride when a bus or subway would do just fine, or a slightly more expensive room. Before you know it, you've wasted ten to twenty dollars a day! And a little care would have saved you one hundred dollars or more, and resulted in an extra three days of relaxation!

The first step in planning a budget is to be realistic. You know how much money is actually there, so now the idea is to spend it wisely. You are not trying to see how little you can spend, if all you wanted to do was to save money, you would have stayed home. A lot of people are so intent upon saving a nickel here and a quarter there that they miss all the fun of their trip. On the other hand, watching money is really important on a vacation because everything in tourist land is set up to get your dollars.

The next step is to consider what is important to you (in other words, where do you want to spend your money?). For some, the important things are luxury hotels and personal transportation. If you will only feel happy staying each night on satin sheets at the Ritz, or riding in taxis to and from all your sightseeing, then budget this in as your main expense, because it will certainly eat up any money you might have wanted to spend on purchases.

Other people prefer to spend their money sightseeing and eating in the best restaurants. Still others look at purchases, things they can take home that will last and remind them of their trip, as the most important item. Whatever you prefer, plan to spend money doing those things, and try to save on the things that are non-essential to you, the less important aspect of your travel.

No matter where you plan to go, the largest expense will be transportation, followed by lodging. Be sure to include service charges and tips when budgeting for hotels. These gratuities add up quickly!

Here are some extra hints worth noting. Read them over before your next trip because any one of them will more than pay for the cost of this book.

1. Drinking tip. Unless you have such finely developed taste buds that anything less than 1959 Rothschild offends you, stick to local beers and wines. They are usually twenty- to fifty percent

cheaper than imports, and sometimes even less. Also, you will find that in Europe, where the locals drink wine every night and not simply on special occasions, they drink the local wines, and seldom splurge on very expensive wines.

2. Hotel hint. On a one-night stay, pass up the room with the bath. The bath, which you probably will not use, depending on the weather of course, can add up to sixty percent of the room's cost. Also, it is a good idea when you are travelling across the European continent, from hotel to hotel, to only schedule yourself into a room with a bath every few days or so. The other days you can use either the hotel bath, or just wash yourself down. Most tourists are so busy that they end up going a bit longer without bathing than they would at home, and there is no reason to pay for it if you're not going to use it.

3. Luggage hint. Avoid leather luggage. It is very heavy and does not hold up. Also, if you are just now buying your luggage to take with you, avoid the heavily constructed types. These weigh many pounds even before you put your belongings in them. You would not want to carry an empty suitcase of this type across an airport or a train station, let alone if it was filled. The best kind of luggage to get, and much cheaper than the above mentioned kind, is the collapsible, cloth or vinyl kind. Be sure, though, to check the zipper—never buy a piece of luggage with a nylon zipper. You know what happens to your clothes with nylon zippers, the teeth spread apart after constant use and you can no longer get the zipper to close. Many times the runner separates and goes off its tracks. The same will happen to your luggage with nylon zippers, but it is very costly to have such a zipper

replaced.

4. Planning tip. Stay away longer. Remember, the biggest expense on any vacation trip is the cost of transportation, especially in getting there and back. If you divide the cost of getting there and returning over ten days, rather than five, your cost per day is halved. Also, unless you stay at least two weeks in your destination, you simply will not get a feel for where you have been. To know the territory and the people, you must stay longer.

Also, use public transportation rather than cabs. This includes buses, trains and trolleys. They may be a bit slower, but they are usually clean, efficient and less than half the price. Look at taxis as emergency vehicles or treats for yourself, and save them for getting to and from train stations and airports (a must!) and for special occasions, like a night out at an expensive club.

5. Luggage hint II. Take less with you. The experienced traveller travels light. I have two friends who travelled through Europe for six months together with a small overnight bag full of clothes for each of them, and they didn't want for anything they had left behind, and they were happy that they didn't have pieces and pieces of luggage to tote off of trains and down the long airport corridors. Carrying a load of possessions with you is solely a state of mind to deal with. There is no necessity involved in bringing five pairs of pants or six dresses with you.

Travelling light not only cuts down on, or completely eliminates your airline overweight charges, which are very high (most airlines will charge you forty dollars for every piece of luggage, no matter what the weight or size, over the amount they allow), but can cut your tips to porters and bellhops significantly. You will not be on display, so it's okay to wear the same dress two days in a row, remember.

6. Eating hint. Make lunch your big meal. In many places, the identical food is served at lunch as at dinner, but at one half the dinner price. Most Europeans eat their largest meal at lunch, anyway, and eat a light dinner. So if you plan on spending seven to ten dollars for lunch, you will be saving at least ten dollars each day and getting the same food for your money.

7. Use the charts below to compare your budgeted cost against actual cost for the first few days. You will quickly learn how realistic your at-home figures were, and whether or not your pocketbook can survive your original plans. If it cannot, do not be ashamed to cut one or two frills, odds are that if you really like the place you're vacationing at, you will return.

DAY 1

	Budget	Actual
Transportation to/from		
Taxis to/from		
Breakfast		
Lunch		
Dinner		
Hotel		
Tips		
Car Rental		
Purchases		
Other (list)		

DAY 2

	Budget	Actual
Transportation to/from		
Taxis to/from		
Breakfast		
Lunch		
Dinner		
Hotel		
Tips		
Car rental		
Purchases		
Other (list)		

XIII

COMING HOME

HOW TO GET YOUR TRIP FOR FREE AFTER YOU RETURN. Uncle Sam says you can write off your trip if you travel on business. This need not mean that you have to buy or sell something. It simply means that you've travelled on business, as in a situation in which you take a "vacation" in a city in which a trade fair and/or exhibition related to your line of work is being held. To find out where these fairs and exhibitions are being held in your field, write to Pan American Airways and ask for their annual book, *Industrial Trade Fairs*. This book is FREE.

Another great move is to claim the trip as an educational expense. If you teach Roman history, a visit to Italy is easily claimed as an educational expense. If you are an American history teacher, chances are almost any trip in the United States can be written off. If you teach French, a trip to France can be written off. Spanish, well a trip to any country speaking Spanish can be totally written off. Remember, save your receipts and keep a daily record of your expenses. A good idea is to purchase an expense record book that you can stick into your back pocket easily, and keep your record in this. Each time you spend any money at all write it down in this book. That way, when it comes time to deal with the tax accountant, you will have all your records neatly logged in.

It is also important to be aware of the taxes you have to pay at your destination. Many countries assess very large fees for sales of certain goods (like automobiles and televisions). Others have significant restaurant taxes which can jack up your bill. Most Central and South American countries charge large nuisance taxes on air tickets purchased for overseas travel, or international travel. These taxes are conspicuously absent from international flights.

COMING THROUGH CUSTOMS. The long and the short of it is that you are allowed to bring in three hundred dollars worth (retail price) of articles purchased overseas, duty-free, if you leave the United States for a vacation. There are certain exceptions to this rule, and there are also ways to partially evade it, but by and large you had better be careful because customs agents around the world are experts.

I have listed some hints, ideas and ways to partially beat the customs agent, although remember, no one can get away, REALLY, with a great deal before the customs agents, and they are very used to people trying.

1. Above all else, remember that customs agents are experts in their field. Regardless of what you may think about a government's political ideas or functional ability, you must realize that customs officials are highly efficient. If you have any ideas about sneaking in a high-priced diamond, forget about it. And, if you've ever regretted not trying to

sneak in that gold watch you thought about because they did not even open your bags, rest assured that they would have, had you tried!

2. Remember, you have to go through customs each time you enter a new country. On the foreign ends of the trip customs officials are primarily concerned with products which command high premiums in their countries, like American cigarettes. In fact, most countries are so concerned about the importation of American brands of cigarettes that they've actually passed special laws dealing with their importation. For example, in most countries, you are allowed to bring in four hundred cigarettes.

The excess will be confiscated in some, but in many others, penalties are more severe. Great Britain's laws mandate that anyone exceeding the limit of four hundred must be charged with an importation tax on all of the cigarettes he/she attempts to bring in (you get nailed, then for the legal four hundred, too, and that tax is a real whopper). You should be especially careful not to try to put anything over on British, Dutch, Greek, Swiss, or Japanese officials. They all take themselves and their jobs very seriously.

One thing about foreign customs officials: the range of treatment they give to travellers is consistent within each country. Austrian, Swiss, Scandinavian, British, Irish, Portugese, Dutch, and Luxembourg officials are courteous and thorough, as are Japanese and most Soviet officials. In sharp contrast are the French, Italian, Spanish, Central and South American, and Eastern Europeans, who are often ill-mannered and nit-picking.

And remember that they are all completely

unpredictable. You never know who they are going to stop, and whose luggage they will want to examine. I remember late one night crossing the Spanish frontier from France. I was on a train, in a compartment with many Algerians who were dressed scruffily, and with two hippie-type students, long hair and dirty clothes, and backpacks. The train was headed for the ultimate destination of the docking point for a cross to Algiers. Because I had boarded the train in Paris directly after a business meeting, I was still in a suit. When we went through customs my bags were the only ones opened!

3. The law says that each person who makes the trip is entitled to bring in three hundred dollars worth of purchases duty-free. This means that your six-week old baby, and your eighty-seven year old grandmother, can also get three hundred dollars worth of duty-free purchases as long as they accompanied you on the trip. Do not fail to take advantage of this, as the three hundred mark is easily passed.

4. Keep your mouth shut. The customs people simply want to get rid of you as quickly as possible, so if you merely answer their questions and save yours for later, you'll get through twice as fast. Also, remember to keep your passport in your hand, open for easy inspection, and speak English, not a foreign language. Don't even try to speak their language. If you are fluent in it, still speak English.

5. You are allowed to bring a maximum of one quart of wine or liquor back with you, duty-free, and you must be more than twenty-one years of age to bring any alcoholic beverages back with you at all.

6. You are allowed to send an unlimited number of gifts, with values of less than ten dollars each,

back to anyone you please, all duty-free. Take advantage of this. Mail as many small items as you can home to friends who will receive them for you. Remember, the duty you pay upon your return will be cumulative for all the things you are carrying with you. Getting many of them out of your hands first is a good idea.

Alcoholic beverages, tobacco, and perfume are not allowed to be sent as gifts, although they often get through. The only other regulation is that no one can receive more than one gift per day. There is probably no way that this can be checked, but just in case, spread out the merchandise to several different friends, to your children, to all of your relatives.

Gifts should be plainly marked:

"UNSOLICITED GIFT. VALUE UNDER TEN DOLLARS"

Now stop and think, how can this be used (misused) to your advantage? Simple. Before you leave make these arrangements with your friends that you will be able to reclaim your gifts when you get home, or buy them from your receivers. Make sure no mention of this practice is made in the package you send, because customs officials do open packages, and if you have noted anything about this in the letter, you may easily be caught.

One other warning: do not allow any merchant to forward your purchase to your home. You may forget to declare it when you return, and be in for stiff penalties. Always buy it yourself and walk down the street to the post office and mail it to a friend at home yourself. You can have the merchant pack it for mailing to make it easier, but never let him mail it.

7. The following things cannot be brought into the United States without special permission of the

Department of Agriculture:

Plants, soils, fruits, vegetables, meats or any other agricultural product.

8. It is also illegal to bring anything in made from animals on the Endangered Species List, absinthe, liquors above the limit, wildlife, lottery tickets, narcotics and drugs which are illegal in the United States, ammunition, and firearms. If you have any doubts or questions, contact the Quarantine Division, United States Department of Agriculture, Federal Center Building, Hyattsville, Maryland.

9. Be sure to declare any foreign-made items you take with you when you leave the United States. This includes your Swiss watch, your English walking cane, Italian shoes, French perfume, Spanish typewriter, etc. Failure to declare them before you leave the United States will probably result in your paying a duty for them when you return.

10. Many times, the things you decide to buy overseas will still be cheaper, after you pay a duty, than they would be if you purchased them here. Remember, merchants and dealers have to pay the same duty you do, and also get hit with transportation, brokerage, and agency fees before adding on their own margin of profit. So you will probably not lose money if you buy it overseas and have to declare it.

11. Be patient when you go through customs. It will often take a long time, and they may not even look at your bag when you finally get to the inspector, but there is absolutely nothing you can say or do about it, so sit back and relax, after all, you are on vacation.

One way to avoid the long customs line is to get to

them first. To do that, if you can check your luggage in last, or near the end of the rest of the passengers, you will usually be the first to get it off the baggage claim people, and then can get through customs before the lines form.

XIV

APPENDICES

PERSONAL RECOMMENDATIONS.
The United States. The Black Hills and Badlands. As far as I am concerned, you really should see America first. It's a true melting pot, with a tremendous variety of cultural heritages. Our landmarks and historic sites will be more meaningful to you and your children, and the people (for the most part) speak English. Travelling around the United States is also good preparation for overseas travel because lifestyles are somewhat different in different sections of the country, but none are totally alien to you.

One travel bargain of the United States which I highly recommend is that part of South Dakota in which you will find the Black Hills and the Badlands. Sites include: Mt. Rushmore, Custer State Park, Wind Cave National Park, Jewel Cave Monument, frontier-tradition cities, etc. The prices are among the lowest in the United States and the weather is great during the spring, summer and fall.

My second American recommendation is the Gold Country in California. This area is located in the foothills of the Sierra Nevada Mountains near

Sacramento in central California. It is the location of the first gold discovery which initiated the Gold Rush of 1849. There are dozens of small towns still in existence, scattered over the countryside. The tradition of the wild west is honored and celebrated each year in many, many festivals in each town. Most of the original gold rush buildings still stand, particularly the hotels, where you can stay in a room, sleeping on a refurbished bed that was first used in that same hotel in the eighteen hundreds by the pioneers. The saloons of that period still abound, and the countryside is lush and beautiful. The hotel prices are quite low, ranging from eight dollars a night for a room sleeping two with full facilities, to thirty dollars for the most deluxe, western suite. Try the National Hotel in Jackson, or the St. George Hotel in my favorite town, Volcano. This is a quiet, lovely vacation spot of the old world charm of the west.

Central America. Guatemala. It's true that almost any Central American nation offers excellent value as far as prices are concerned, largely because the American dollar is worth an awful lot down there. But Central America is a part of the world filled with its own problems, ranging from unstable governments to earthquakes, unsanitary cities to tepid jungles, and particularly today, to revolutions. I highly recommend, however, Guatemala, as one of the great unspoiled locations in Central America. The Indians and the Spanish people mingle together in this nation, the crafts are particularly interesting, such as weaving, knitting, pottery, and wood-carving, and the government has been one of the most stable lately.

I recommend that you do not go to Nicaragua, El Salvador or Belize, as these governments are quite unpredictable.

In Guatemala, though, the exchange rate is relatively good, the economy half-way decent, and it offers a solid combination of modern cities, Spanish tradition, Indian heritage, beaches, and jungle.

South America. Peru. For the traveller looking for the best deal in South America, Peru is the place to go. The Peruvian Sol makes the exchange rate quite good now. You can get an inexpensive, complete, day-long tour of the capital city, Lima, and for a few cents more they will throw in a huge lunch and dinner that you will not soon forget. The food in Peru is great, and quite interesting as a change from the normal Hispanic dishes. The most expensive restaurant in the country charges only half the price of the most expensive Mexican restaurant in Mexico City, and serves for this amount a complete dinner which three people couldn't finish.

In Peru you will find the jungles of the Andes valleys, and ruins from a variety of civilizations, most notably, Machu Pichu, the ruins of the ancient Indian civilization which settled the top of a mountain. The view from this location is truly breathtaking, and is one of the most awe-inspiring views I have ever seen.

Europe. Spain. You can search far and wide, up and down all of this continent, and you'll find no better vacation value than Spain, especially the Costa del Sol on its southern shores. Temperatures are ideal from April until October, and humidity rarely exceeds seventy percent.

Here you will find groves of olive trees and orange trees spreading out to the beautiful blue Mediterranean sea, Moorish architecture left over from a civilization of prophets who conquered

Spain in the eight hundreds, and the subtle European architecture which filtered in over the Pyrenees Mountains from France. You will find countless separate cultures in Spain, from the Basque country people to the Catalonian rebels to the Castilian aristocracy. All fascinating, and all inexpensive tours ready for you to take.

The history of Spain is glorious, and so is the nation today. Excellent exchange rate increases this super value.

Africa. Kenya. Its capital city is stunningly modern, yet fifteen minutes away, and you can see lions on the loose. Exchange rate here is good to the United States dollar and the country offers safaris, European-style night life, etc. One of the interesting features of Kenya is that the country has been only lately developed with modern buildings and consequently the architecture is nothing but the most modern styles; and this against the background of a land as yet further developed, a rich and primitive land, is quite breathtaking.

Far East. Macao. The big bargain out there, largely because of its Portugese ownership, keeping the exchange rate at rock bottom prices. There is a unique blend in this city of Chinese culture, island life, Portugese culture, and all sorts of attractions are offered and mixed in this exciting atmosphere. Gambling is a big event here, as well as many recreational activities. Don't drink the water, whatever you do, and don't drink mixed drinks with ice cubes in them.

For the souvenir hunter, Macao is a great bargain because everything is cheaper here than in Hong Kong, Singapore, Japan, or Taiwan.

Asia. Mongolia. Somewhat expensive to get to, but it is well worth it in terms of uniqueness. The capital city of Mongolia is Ulan Bator, and is the only city in the whole country. The population of Mongolia is one and a half million people, most nomad or agricultural.

Needless to say, in a country such as this, your dollar will go much farther. Be sure to get the necessary visas in advance to your entry into this country.

The food in Mongolia is quite inexpensive, and very different. I guarantee that you will never have tasted anything like Mongolian food before. It is a mixture of Russian, Chinese, and Arabic, with imported European subtleties.

This is the land of Genghis Khan, the Gobi Desert, etc. There is no night life to speak of, though, and you should be prepared to entertain yourself with sightseeing and countryside travel during the days. There are no clubs, casinos, etc., to throw money away in.

DOWN UNDER. Tasmania. Australia is a nice place to visit for Americans, with a solid exchange rate and a liking for us. But my personal opinion of Australia is that you might as well stay at home: the Australians live just like we do, with the exception of their penchant for pub-crawling, and for that, one might as well go to England.

However, the one place Down Under that I do find enchanting, is the island of Tasmania. It is the least inhabited civilized section of Australia, and it offers many strange sights, including an eerie old prison, casinos, beaches that are unmatched in California, etc. This is really a unique bargain.

SAVINGS IN ENGLAND. Each year, thousands of Americans travel to Merry Old England. The English pound has been suffering of late, and the country is still in a state of depression, so the English are out to get as many tourist dollars as they can. Prices have soured in England to the point of unrecognizability. You will pay in pence and pounds in England what you would pay in dollars and cents here: in other words, you will be paying twice the aount for items, be they food stuffs, drinks, or clothing, as you would in the United States.

The cost of touring England has skyrocketed, but there are still many bargains for the smart traveller.

Let's start with transportation. The English subways and buses are inexpensive and clean. They are also quite safe. Personally, I prefer the buses, because you get to see quite a bit of the city that way, and London is a lovely city to look at, filled with parks and clean buildings (after the great "building-wash"). However, the undergrounds, or "tubes" as they are called, are fast and efficient. They are, though, going up this year in price, so you might want to get to know the bus system, which is not so expensive.

If it's sightseeing that catches your interest in London, there are a couple of buses which will take you on tours for only a couple of pounds (about five dollars). These tours are pleasant, you ride in double decker buses, and there is a constant, charming commentary on the sights by the guide. You can catch these "Around London" tours at Grosvenor Gardens near Victoria Station. Also available are certain normal bus routes which happen to tour in particularly interesting areas. Take the Number 3 bus from its northern terminal in Camden Town and ride south to the Crystal Palace. The cost is less than one dollar, the bus is the old-style double-decker, and the sights along the way include: Regent's Park, Trafalgar Square, Buckingham

Palace, Admiralty Arch, Westminster Abbey and the Houses of Parliament, the National Recreation Center, and the London Zoo.

Another interesting bus ride to take is the 14. Catch this on Charing Cross Road in front of Foyle's Book Store and take it toward Cambridge Circus and Picadilly Circus. This bus will tour you all over the central shopping district of London, through the West End, and down to Knightsbridge and Hyde Park. Again, the cost is minimal, about eighty cents, and the ride is fascinating.

And remember, the best place for sightseeing on these buses is the top deck, but it is also the smoking section.

There are dozens of localized cruises and country jaunts which will save you many dollars. Just check the Yellow Pages and commerce centers, the holiday listings of the Guardian newspaper, or the holiday listings of Time Out magazine for more information on the types of sights you'd like to see in London.

One of my favorite out of London vacation spots is the Cornish coast. The home of King Arthur and the many legends surrounding him, Cornwall is both beautiful with lush, green countryside and spectacular sea views, and inexpensive. Try the town of St. Austell on the southern coast, or Mevagissey or Tintagel. Each has a distinction all its own, each offers rooms for ten dollars a night, and each has houses available to be rented at the low price of eighty dollars a week! The food in this area is quite cheap, and the entertainment, too, for all you need to do for a full night of entertainment is walk down to the local pub for a game of darts and a pint with some of the locals. They will tell you stories of the romantic history of Cornwall, or mystery stories of spies during World War II.

Cornwall is located about a day's drive or train trip from London. The railway connections are quite easy to make from the city, as trains leave frequently. The high season in this beach resort, known to the English as the "Riviera of England", is of course, during the summer, because the weather is sunny and mild. However, the autumn and winter are also lovely times to visit.

Another great value is the British "Open to View" pass, good for free or discount admission to more than four hundred fascinating places like Stonehenge, Warwick Castle, Windsor Castle, and many more. The pass costs just a few dollars, and is good for one month. Another advantage: you can merely show the pass at the door and you're in—no waiting in line! For more information, contact your local British Rail (Britrail) office.

And if you decide to add a stop in Paris, there are many discount flights from London to the French city. Typically, students can obtain discounts of sixty to seventy-five percent. And these kinds of bargains are also extended to flights to Tel Aviv, Nairobi, Bangkok and several other desirable cities.

As for food in the English countryside, there are dozens of super eating spots in the small towns and along the roads, where you can still get excellent meals for two to seven dollars. Try the pub lunches while you are travelling. You can find them for as little as three dollars, and you'll be getting a world of atmosphere, as well, because the country pubs in England are some of the oldest buildings on the island. Another good food buy while you are driving, busing or training around the countryside, are cream teas. These are a tradition in southern England, and are, of course, served at teatime, around three or four o'clock. They are huge meals, nothing with a main course, though, but the quantity of food served is enormous for the price, usually about three dollars.

So travel, eat, drink, and enjoy England—and save while you're doing it!

THE MIDDLE EAST. Alexandria, Egypt. Even in this day of social and political unrest around the world, one of the most beautiful and charming cities to behold is Alexandria. Established by Alexander the Great in ancient times, many of the streets are still the original ones which he mapped out. Middle Easterners call this city the Paris of the Middle East. Because of the great influx of Greeks, Turks, and French, this city is the most cosmopolitan in the Middle East today (the other cosmopolitan city being Beirut, which of course, you should steer clear of because of the constant and long-lasting civil war raging there). The night life in Alexandria is phenomenal. You can find the most sophisticated singers, dancers, and bands, as well as authentic Arab music, if you are looking for the old world culture. The city itself is located on the Mediterranean sea, at the delta of the Nile, and just as the river meets the sea, so meets several cultures and several centuries in this city. The beaches here are spectacular, the sunsets breathtaking. The prices can't be beat, even in this time of boosted tourism in Egypt.

Of course, if you go to visit Alexandria, you shouldn't leave Egypt without taking a trip down the Nile to visit the pyramids and the Great Sphynx.

Israel. Though the inflation rate in Israel is higher than our own, I would still recommend it, if not for bargains, then for the history that this Jewish homeland is rich in. There is so much to see in the Land of Abraham, Isaac, and Jacob, that prices will never slow the flood of tourists who make their way to the Land the followers of Moses, Jesus, and Mohammed call their Holy Land.

Lebanon was a real bargain until she was torn apart by the recent civil war; Saudi Arabia and the United Arab Emirates are extremely expensive; and Jordan is unsafe for Americans. I would also avoid Syria and Iraq, as they are both openly anti-American.

However, Tunisia is a fine spot for vacationing on the beaches. It is quite inexpensive, and is very popular with Europeans. Morocco is still charming and old world, even with the great recent influx of tourists, and I would not miss it on a trip to the Middle East. The charm and beauty of the white-washed houses in Casablanca are unbeatable, and the leather goods and Middle Eastern fashions are of the highest quality there, as is the brass carving done in Morocco.

APPENDIX II.

GUIDES. Every year federal and state governments spend millions of dollars on information services. These expenditures are supplemented by local chambers of commerce, and services provided by town Rotary, Kiwanis, and other organizations. Many large corporations and trade associations also spend large sums on travel guides to lure the public to new areas of growth, or as tax-deductible "public service" publications.

Here is a list of FREE books, guides, maps, and charts offered by a variety of organizations and governments. They are all worth writing for, and you need not mention this publication to obtain them. Simply write to the address given and ask for a copy of the product mentioned.

National Parks Activities Guides. Free directory of every National Park and Monument, complete with descriptions and ordering information. Write to the Manager, Public Documents Distribution Center, 5801 Tabor Avenue, Philadelphia, Pennsylvania 19120.

Pennsylvania Dutch Country Guides. Free vacation booklets, courtesy of the Pennsylvania Dutch Tourist Bureau, 1800 Hempstead Road, Lancaster, Pennsylvania 17601.

Guide to Georgia's Historic Homes. A thirty-one page free guide to historic homesites in the Peach

State. Contact Ed Garrett, Department of Industry and Trade, Tourist Division, Post Office Box 38097, Atlanta Georgia.

Woodbridge Center Shopper's Guide. An illustrated guide to the largest shopping mall in the East. Write to Woodbridge Area Chamber of Commerce, 655 Amboy Avenue, Woodbridge, New Jersey 07095.

Geological Survey State Maps. For some of the most accurate and beautiful maps of the United States, write to the United States Geological Survey, Distribution Section, Washington, D.C. 20242. Ask for any or all states.

America's Famous Dams and Reservoirs. Write to the Bureau of Reclamation, Engineering and Research Center, Building 67, Denver Federal Center, Denver, Colorado 80225.

Every state offers a vacation guide, with many additional pamphlets filled with information about specific intrastate areas of interest. Simply write to the Tourist Bureau or Chamber of Commerce of the state or states you are interested in, and something should be forthcoming.

For states, a typical address might be: New Hampshire Office of Vacation Travel, Box 856, Concord, New Hampshire, 03301.

For cities: Boulder Chamber of Commerce, 1101 Canyon, Boulder, Colorado 80302.

Here are some additional listings:

Washington, D.C. Pocket Guide to Eating. Write to Washington Convention and Visitors Bureau, 1129 Twentieth Street, Northwest, Washington, D.C. 20036.

Rhode Island Tourist Guide. Write to Rhode Island Developmental Council, Tourist Promotion Division, Williams Building, Hayes Street,

Providence, Rhode Island 02908.

Cape Cod Resort Directory. Write for this sixty-five page booklet listing the best values, to Cape Cod Chamber of Commerce, Hyannis, Maryland 02601.

Winston-Salem Vacation Kits. Write to the Greater Winston-Salem Chamber of Commerce, Box 1408, Winston-Salem, North Carolina 27102.

Oregon Full-Color Vacation Guide. Write to the Oregon State Highway Division, Travel Information Director, Highway Building, Room 104, Salem, Oregon 97310.

Tennessee Country Musicland. Write to the Nashville Area Chamber of Commerce, Convention and Visitors Division, Department Q, 161 Fourth Avenue, North, Nashville, Tennessee 37219.

Dinosaur Land—Glen Rose, Texas. This is a wonderful and fascinating vacationland in the home of the Dinosaur. Write to the Glen Rose Somervell County, the Chamber of Commerce, Glen Rose, Texas 76043.

Senior Citizens Driving Guide. Write to the American Optometric Association, at 7000 Chippewa Street, St. Louis, Missouri 63119. Ask for "Driving Tips for Senior Citizens."

Idaho Winter Vacation Guide. Write to the Idaho Department of Commerce and Development, Capitol Building, Room 108, Boise, Idaho 83707.

Tri-State Rodeo Fact Sheet. Write for this to the Fort Madison Rodeo Corporation, 835-1/2G, Fort Madison, Iowa 52627.

The Salinas Rodeo—The Biggest Rodeo in the West. Write for this information to the Salinas Rodeo Committee, Salinas Chamber of Commerce, Main Street, Salinas, California.

Delmarva Peninsula Vacation Guides. The Delmarva Peninsula combines Delaware, Maryland, and Virginia. Write for information to the Salisbury Area Chamber of Commerce, Post Office Box 510, Salisbury, Maryland 21801.

APPENDIX III.

Tourist Offices Around the World. Here are some words to the wise. Before you go, write! Tourist offices have an immense body of information, from dates and accommodation information about festivals, seasonal activities, roads, products, historical facts. Months before you go on a trip, you should sit down and write. You'll know more about where you are going and enjoy your trip more. A short letter that asks for guidebooks or maps will bring a flood of materials. Below is a list of tourist agencies that were created to help make your trip more interesting.

Antiqua. The Antiqua Tourist Information Office, Box 363, St. John's, Antiqua, British West Indies.

Argentina. Direccion Nacional de Turismo, Uruquay No. 291, Buenos Aires, Argentina.

Aruba. The Aruba Information Center, 1270 Avenue of the Americas, New York, New York.

Australia. Australian National Tourist Association, 636 Fifth Avenue, New York, New York 10020.

Austria. Austrian State Tourist Department, 545 Fifth Avenue, New York, New York 10017.

Bahamas. Bahamas Ministry of Tourism, 620 Fifth Avenue, New York, New York 10020.

Barbados. Barbados Consul General, 800 Second

Avenue, New York, New York.

Belgium. Belgian Consul General, 50 Rockefeller Plaza, New York, New York.

Bermuda. Bermuda Government Official Travel Information Office, 630 Fifth Avenue, New York, New York 10020.

Bolivia. Bolivian Consul General, 10 Rockefeller Plaza, New York, New York.

Bonaire. Bonaire Information Center, 685 Fifth Avenue, New York, New York.

Brazil. Brazilian Government Trade Bureau, 630 Fifth Avenue, New York, New York.

Britain. British Tourist Authority, 680 Fifth Avenue, New York, New York 10019.

Bulgaria. Bulgarian Tourist Office, 50 East Forty-second Street, New York, New York.

Canada. Canadian Government Travel Bureau, 1251 Avenue of the Americas, New York, New York.

Caribbean. Eastern Caribbean Travel Association, 220 East Forty-second Street, New York, New York.

Ceylon. Ceylon Tourist Boad, 609 Fifth Avenue, New York, New York.

Chile. Chilean Trade Bureau, 277 Park Avenue, New York, New York.

Columbia. Columbia National Tourist Board, 10 East Forty-sixth Street, New York, New York

Costa Rica. Costa Rican Tourist Office, 630 Fifth Avenue, New York, New York.

Curacao. Curacao Information Center, 685 Fifth Avenue, New York, New York.

Cyprus. Cyprus Mission to the United Nations, 820 Second Avenue, New York, New York.

Denmark. Danish National Travel Office, 280 Park Avenue, New York, New York.

Dominican Republic. Dominican Republic Tourist Office, 485 Madison Avenue, New York, New York.

Ecuador. Ecuadorean Tourist Office, 167 West Seventy-second Street, New York, New York.

Egypt. Egyptian Government Tourist Office, 630 Fifth Avenue, New York, New York.

Finland. Finnish National Travel Office, 540 Madison Avenue, New York, New York.

Fiji. Fiji Mission to the United Nations, 1 United Nations Plaza, New York, New York.

France. French Government Tourist Office, 610 Fifth Avenue, New York, New York 10020.

French West Indies. Tourist Board of the French West Indies, 610 Fifth Avenue, New York, New York.

Germany. German Tourist Information Office, 630 Fifth Avenue, New York, New York.

Grenada. Grenada Tourist Information Office, 141 East Forty-fourth Street, New York, New York.

Guatemala. Guatemalan Mission to the United Nations, 405 Lexington Avenue, New York, New York.

Greece. Greek Consulate General's Office, 69 East Seventy-ninth Street, New York, New York.

Haiti. Haiti Government Tourist Bureau, 30 Rockefeller Plaza, New York, New York.

Honduras. Honduras Information Service, 501 Fifth Avenue, New York, New York.

Hong Kong. Hong Kong Tourist Association, 548 Fifth Avenue, New York, New York.

Hungary. Hungarian Consul General, 8 East Seventy-fifth Street, New York, New York.

Iceland. Icelandic Consul General's Office, 370 Lexington Avenue, New York, New York.

India. Indian Consul General's Office, 3 East 64th

Street, New York, New York.

Indonesia. Consulate General of Indonesia Information Service, 5 East 68th Street, New York, New York 10021.

Iraq. Iraq Mission to the United Nations, 14 East Seventy-ninth Street, New York, New York.

Ireland. Irish Tourist Board, 590 Fifth Avenue, New York, New York, 10036.

Israel. Israeli Consul General's Office, 800 Second Avenue, New York, New York.

Italy. Italian Consul General's Office, 690 Park Avenue, New York, New York.

Italian Cultural Institute, 686 Park Avenue, New York, New York.

Jamaica. Jamaica Tourist Board, 2 Dag Hammerskjold Plaza, New York, New York.

Japan. Japan National Tourist Organization, 45 Rockefeller Center, New York, New York 10020.

Kenya. Kenya Mission to the United Nations. 866 United Nations Plaza, New York, New York.

Lebanon, Lebanon Consul General's Office, 9 East Seventy-sixth Street, New York, New York.

Luxembourg. Luxembourg Tourist Department, 1 Dag Hammerskjold Plaza, New York, New York.

Malta. Malta Mission to the United Nations, 249 East Thirty-fifth Street, New York, New York.

Martinique. French Government Tourist Office, 610 Fifth Avenue, New York, New York 10020.

Mexico. Mexican National Tourist Council, 405 Park Avenue, New York, New York.

Monaco. Monaco Consul General's Office, 20 East Forty-ninth Street, New York, New York.

Morocco. Moroccan National Tourist Office, 521 Fifth Avenue, New York, New York.

Netherlands. Netherlands Consul General's Office, 1 Rockefeller Plaza, New York, New York.

New Zealand. New Zealand Government Travel Commissioner, 630 Fifth Avenue, New York, New York 10020.

Norway. Norwegian National Travel Office, 800 Third Avenue, New York, New York.

Pakistan. Pakistani Consul General's Office, 12 East Sixty-fifth Avenue, New York, New York.

Panama. Panamanian Government Tourist Bureau, 630 Fifth Avenue, New York, New York 10020.

Paraguay. Paraguay Mission to the United Nations, 211 East Forty-third Street, New York, New York.

Peru. Peruvian Mission to the United Nations, 10 Rockefeller Plaza, New York, New York.

Philippines. Philippine Tourist and Travel Association, 556 Fifth Avenue, New York, New York.

Poland. Polish Travel Office (Orbis), 500m Fifth Avenue, New York, New York 10036.

Puerto Rico. Commonwealth of Puerto Rico, Department of Tourism, 1290 Avenue of the Americas, New York, New York.

Portugal. Portuguese Information and Tourist Office, 548 Fifth Avenue, New York, New York.

Quebec, Province of Quebec, Department of Tourism, 17 West Fiftieth Street, New York, New York 10020.

Romania. Romanian Trade Office, 200 East Thirty-eighth Street, New York, New York.

St. Maarten. Netherlands Windward Islands Information Center, 445 Park Avenue, New York, New York.

St. Lucia. St. Lucia Tourist Information Office, 220 East Forty-second Street, New York, New York.

San Marino. San Marino Consul General's Office, 400 Madison Avenue, New York, New York.

Saudi Arabia. Saudi Arabian Information Service, 866 United Nations Plaza, New York, New York.

Senegal. Senegalese Tourist Information Office, 200 Park Avenue, New York, New York.

Singapore. Singapore Government Tourist Information Office, 342 Madison Avenue, New York, New York.

Somalia. Somalian Mission to the United Nations, 747 Third Avenue, New York, New York.

Spain. Spanish National Tourist Office, 665 Fifth Avenue, New York, New York.

Sudan. Sudanese Mission to the United Nations, 210 East Forty-ninth Street, New York, New York.

Surinam. Surinam Tourist Bureau, 1 United Nations Plaza, New York, New York.

Sweden. Swedish National Travel Office, 75 Rockefeller Plaza, New York, New York.

Switzerland. Swiss National Tourist Office, 608 Fifth Avenue, New York, New York 10020.

Syria. Syrian Permanent Mission to the United Nations, 964 Third Avenue, New York, New York.

Thailand. Tourist Organization of Thailand, Five World Trade Center, New York, New York.

Togo. Togoland Mission to the United Nations, 112 East Fortieth Street, New York, New York.

Trinidad and Tobago. Tourist Board and Information Service of Trinidad and Tobago, 420 Lexington Avenue, New York, New York.

Tunisia. Tunisian Trade and Tourist Office, 630 Fifth Avenue, New York, New York.

Turkey. Turkish Consul General's Office, 821 United Nations Plaza, New York, New York.

Union of Soviet Socialist Republics. Soviet

Intourist Bureau, the Official Tourist Bureau of the Soviet Union. 630 Fifth Avenue, New York, New York.

United Kingdom. The Trade Office of the United Kingdom, 150 East 58th Street, New York, New York.

Uruguay. The Consul General's Office of Uruguay, 301 East Forty-seventh Street, New York, New York.

Venezuela. Venezuelan Government Tourist Bureau, 450 Park Avenue, New York, New York.

Virgin Islands. The Virgin Islands Government Information Center, 16 West Forty-ninth Street, New York, New York 10020.

Yugoslavia. Yugoslav State Tourist Office, 854 Fifth Avenue, New York, New York.